THE ECONOMICS
of
TRADE UNIONS

CAMBRIDGE ECONOMIC HANDBOOKS

Edited by

C. W. GUILLEBAUD, *St. John's College, Cambridge*

and

MILTON FRIEDMAN, *University of Chicago*

Initiated by the late John Maynard Keynes and continued under the successive editorships of D. H. Robertson and C. W. Guillebaud, the Cambridge Economic Handbooks are, in Lord Keynes's words, "intended to convey to the ordinary reader and to the uninitiated student some conception of the general principles of thought which economists now apply to economic problems." The series is now edited jointly by Mr. Guillebaud and Mr. Friedman in order to bring the best American as well as British economic thinking to bear on the major problems of economics in both countries.

The Economics of Under-developed Countries
By PETER T. BAUER *and* BASIL S. YAMEY

International Economics
By ROY F. HARROD

Supply and Demand
By HUBERT HENDERSON

The Business Cycle
By R. C. O. MATTHEWS

Money
By D. H. ROBERTSON

The Structure of Competitive Industry
By E. A. G. ROBINSON

The Economics of Trade Unions
By ALBERT REES

BY ALBERT REES

THE ECONOMICS
of
TRADE UNIONS

THE UNIVERSITY OF CHICAGO PRESS

This book is also available in a clothbound edition from

THE UNIVERSITY OF CHICAGO PRESS

Published by The University of Chicago Press in association with
James Nisbet & Co. Ltd. and The Cambridge University Press

The University of Chicago Press, Chicago 60637
James Nisbet & Co. Ltd., Digswell Place, Welwyn, England
The Macmillan Company of Canada, Toronto 2

INTRODUCTION

TO THE CAMBRIDGE ECONOMIC HANDBOOKS

BY THE GENERAL EDITORS

Soon after the war of 1914–18 there seemed to be a place for a series of short introductory handbooks, "intended to convey to the ordinary reader and to the uninitiated student some conception of the general principles of thought which economists now apply to economic problems."

This Series was planned and edited by the late Lord Keynes under the title "Cambridge Economic Handbooks" and he wrote for it a General Editorial Introduction of which the words quoted above formed part. In 1936 Keynes handed over the editorship of the Series to Mr. D. H. Robertson, who held it till 1946, when he was succeeded by Mr. C. W. Guillebaud.

It was symptomatic of the changes which had been taking place in the inter-war period in the development of economics, changes associated in a considerable measure with the work and influence of Keynes himself, that within a few years the text of part of the Editorial Introduction should have needed revision. In its original version the last paragraph of the Introduction ran as follows:

"Even on matters of principle there is not yet a complete unanimity of opinion amongst professional economists. Generally speaking, the writers of these volumes believe themselves to be orthodox members of the Cambridge School of Economics. At any rate, most of their ideas about the subject, and even their prejudices, are traceable to the contact they have enjoyed with the writings and lectures of the two economists who have chiefly influenced Cambridge thought for the past fifty years, Dr. Marshall and Professor Pigou."

Keynes later amended this concluding paragraph to read:

"Even on matters of principle there is not yet a complete unanimity of opinion amongst professional students of the subject. Immediately after the war (of 1914–18) daily economic events were of such a startling character as to divert attention from theoretical complexities. But today, economic science has recovered its wind. Traditional treatments and traditional solutions are being questioned, improved and revised. In the end this activity of research should clear up controversy. But for the moment controversy and doubt are increased. The writers of this Series must apologize to the general reader and to the beginner if many parts of their subject have not yet reached to a degree of certainty and lucidity which would make them easy and straightforward reading."

Many though by no means all the controversies which Keynes had in mind when he penned these words have since been resolved. The new ideas and new criticisms, which then seemed to threaten to overturn the old orthodoxy, have, in the outcome, been absorbed within it and have served rather to strengthen and deepen it, by adding needed modifications and changing emphasis, and by introducing an altered and on the whole more precise terminology. The undergrowth which for a time concealed that main stream of economic thought to which Keynes referred in his initial comment and to which he contributed so greatly has by now been largely cleared away so that there is again a large measure of agreement among economists of all countries on the fundamental theoretical aspects of their subject.

This agreement on economic analysis is accompanied by wide divergence of views on questions of economic policy. These reflect both different estimates of the quantitative importance of one or another of the conflicting forces involved in any prediction about the consequences of a policy measure and different value judgments about the desirability of the predicted outcome. It still remains as true today as it was when Keynes wrote that—to quote once more from his Introduction:

> "The Theory of Economics does not furnish a body of settled conclusions immediately applicable to policy. It is a method rather than a doctrine, an apparatus of the mind, a technique of thinking, which helps its possessor to draw correct conclusions."

This method, while in one sense eternally the same, is in another ever changing. It is continually being applied to new problems raised by the continual shifts in policy views. This is reflected in the wide range of topics covered by the Cambridge Economic Handbooks already published, and in the continual emergence of new topics demanding coverage. Such a series as this should accordingly itself be a living entity, growing and adapting to the changing interests of the times, rather than a fixed number of essays on a set plan.

The wide welcome given to the Series has amply justified the judgment of its founder. Apart from its circulation in the British Empire, it has been published from the start in the United States of America, and translations of the principal volumes have appeared in a number of foreign languages.

The present change to joint Anglo-American editorship is designed to increase still further the usefulness of the Series by expanding the range of potential topics, authors and readers alike. It will succeed in its aim if it enables us to bring to a wide audience on both sides of the Atlantic lucid explanations and significant applications of "that technique of thinking" which is the hallmark of economics as a science.

C. W. GUILLEBAUD
MILTON FRIEDMAN

PREFACE

MOST of this book was written while I was a Fellow of the Center for Advanced Study in the Behavioral Sciences, Stanford, California. I am deeply grateful to the Center for providing me a year of complete freedom from routine duties to be spent in surpassingly beautiful surroundings and with stimulating colleagues; without such an opportunity, this book would not have been undertaken.

A draft manuscript was read by Milton Friedman, C. W. Guillebaud, H. Gregg Lewis, Melvin W. Reder, and George P. Shultz, each of whom made many valuable suggestions. Needless to say, none of them is responsible for any remaining errors, nor does any of them necessarily share the value judgments I have expressed.

The book is entitled "The Economics of Trade Unions" to avoid any pretense of offering a complete treatment of unions as institutions. The emphasis on economic aspects is in keeping with the traditions of the Cambridge Economic Handbooks. Nevertheless, I have included some material on unions as political institutions toward the end of the book. Readers who lack any background in the institutional aspects of American unions may prefer to read Chapter X after Chapter I.

The final chapter is an evaluation of American unions that attempts to take into account both economic and non-economic aspects. Since the methods and preoccupations of economics strictly defined may tend to predispose the economist toward an unfavorable view of trade unions, the reader will want to keep in mind that this final broadening of perspective will appreciably alter some of the evaluations implicit in much of the earlier material.

CHICAGO   A. R.

CONTENTS

CHAPTER I

INSTITUTIONAL FRAMEWORK

CHAPTER II

THE SOURCES OF UNION POWER

CHAPTER III

UNION WAGE POLICY

CHAPTER IV

THE INFLUENCE OF UNIONS ON RELATIVE EARNINGS

CHAPTER V

UNIONS AND THE GENERAL LEVEL OF WAGES AND PRICES

CHAPTER VI

ENTRY TO UNIONS AND UNION SECURITY

CHAPTER VII

UNION PRACTICES AFFECTING EMPLOYMENT AND PRODUCTIVITY

CHAPTER VIII

SENIORITY

CHAPTER IX

GRIEVANCE PROCEDURES

CHAPTER X

THE UNION AS A POLITICAL INSTITUTION

CHAPTER XI

CORRUPTION IN UNIONS

CHAPTER XII

EVALUATION AND PREDICTION

INDEX

TABLES

FIGURE

CHAPTER I

INSTITUTIONAL FRAMEWORK

§1. The Character of American Unions. Trade unions are highly complex and diverse institutions. Because they are so complex, they can profitably be studied from the standpoint of several disciplines, including economics, political science, sociology, and history. An account from any one point of view will, like this one, necessarily be incomplete. Because unions are so diverse, it is hard to generalize about them, and any generalizations made will have exceptions that cannot be enumerated in a small book.

The problems raised by the complexity and diversity of unions can, however, be minimized by focusing the discussion on American unions of the present day. These, though still diverse, are less so than in some earlier periods, and their economic aspects are of central importance For the United States we can consider trade unions as a self-contained set of institutions. In many other countries we would have to consider unions as one part of a closely-knit tripartite labor movement whose other two parts are the consumer co-operatives and a labor or a Socialist political party. But the United States now has no labor party and no Socialist party of any importance. American consumer co-operatives have no close links with trade unions—they are characteristic of farm areas, university towns, and a dwindling number of relatively homogeneous immigrant communities.

Socialism was once an important force in American unionism, and vestiges of its influence remain. However, all important

1

American unions now accept and work within a system of modified capitalism or free enterprise. They have views on the desirable evolution of this system, but they do not seek to change it radically, either by peaceful or violent means. The union leader who said "unions are for capitalism for the same reason that fish are for water" could only have been an American. It has been many years since a union of any importance would, as the Industrial Workers of the World did, inscribe on its banner the revolutionary watchword "Abolition of the Wage System" or publish a book of *Songs To Fan the Flames of Discontent.*

It would be interesting to speculate on why the United States is the only important country whose labor movement has no Socialist, syndicalist, or religious ideology. The rapid rise in the living standards of American workers, the relative ease of geographical and occupational mobility, the long history of universal franchise and free public education may all play a part. But such speculation would take us too far afield. The crucial point is that in the absence of a dominating radical or religious doctrine, economic activities are central to American labor unions. These activities can be studied with the tools of economic analysis.

The prevailing spirit of the American union movement is often summed up in the descriptive phrase "business unionism" as contrasted with "radical unionism" or "uplift unionism." The term business unionism should not be considered a term of derogation, and it does not mean that the union has the same goals as a profit business. Rather it means that the union is primarily, though not exclusively, engaged in advancing the interests of its members through seeking improvements in their own wages, hours, and working conditions, and is only secondarily concerned with broader programs of social reform.

In some of their economic activities, professional associations may closely resemble trade unions, although such organizations as the American Medical Association and the American Association of University Professors do not consider themselves unions. Such organizations will be excluded from the discussion of this book unless explicit notice is given to the contrary. Like most boundaries, that between unions and union-like organizations is hard to draw with precision. Though some professional associations are entirely concerned with advancing knowledge or improving the competence of their members, others take an active interest in the economic status of their profession. Two characteristics are most nearly distinctive, though shared by a few organizations affiliated with the trade union movement. First, many professional associations include self-employed persons, executives, or employers among their members. Second, professional associations seldom engage in collective bargaining and do not strike.

It is perhaps unnecessary to give a formal definition of a union, since unions are as well known to any inhabitant of the modern world as the words that can be used to define them. However, a definition of its subject gives a book an air of decorum, and the preceding discussion permits a definition here. American trade unions are associations of employees (usually wage-earners) that seek to improve the economic position of their members primarily by bargaining with employers within the broad framework of the existing economic system.

§ 2. **Historical Sketch.** Trade unions in the United States are almost as old as the Republic. Organizations of printers and shoemakers existed in Philadelphia and New York before 1800, and one of the first recorded strikes was conducted by Philadelphia printers in 1786.[1] The early unions were confined to the largest cities because only there were more than a few employees concentrated in the same trade. Organization took place first among the skilled for two main reasons: these

[1] Selig Perlman, *A History of Trade Unionism in the United States* (New York: Macmillan Co., 1923), pp. 3–4. There is not complete agreement among labor historians on the date of the first union and the first strike, since it is hard to classify some of the ephemeral organizations and amorphous labor disturbances of the early period.

workers had the education needed to form and run a union (a factor especially important in the case of printers), and they had a firm commitment to their trades made by investing in specialized skills as apprentices. The unskilled worker was less concerned with improving his lot through organization because he could hope to better himself through mobility—upward occupationally or outward to the geographical frontier.

The early unions met with hostility from both the masters and the courts. In the celebrated Philadelphia cordwainers' case of 1806 (cordwainer is an old term for shoemaker) the courts found a strike for higher piece rates to be a criminal conspiracy at common law. In the following years, strikers were convicted on similar charges in several Eastern states. The tradition was not breached until 1842 in the Massachusetts case *Commonwealth* vs. *Hunt*, which foreshadowed the doctrine that the legality of a strike depends on its purpose.

Throughout their early history, American unions were severely affected by economic depressions. Not only did reduced employment cut the number of members, but employers often took advantage of loose labor markets to refuse to pay union wage scales or to discharge union members. The depression that followed the end of the Napoleonic Wars wiped out many of the union organizations of the time. After 1820, however, unionization spread to other trades, including hatters, tailors, weavers, and carpenters.

Until the 1820's, each local craft union had been a separate organization. The year 1827 can be said to mark the beginning of a labor movement, for in that year the first federation of local unions was formed in Philadelphia. An organization of local unions in the same city without regard to craft or industry is now called a "city central," a form of organization that still exists (*e.g.* the Chicago Federation of Labor). Because of its diverse composition, a city central cannot be concerned with collective bargaining problems, though it can offer sympathetic support to local unions engaged in strikes and can function as the voice of unions in civic affairs. This was, indeed, the function of the original Philadelphia organization, which called for the election of candidates representing workingmen. In the following years, workingmen's parties were organized in Philadelphia, New York, and Boston, and fought for such objectives as free public education and the enactment of mechanics' lien laws. Although these objectives were soon achieved, the political parties themselves quickly disappeared.

During the early 1830's, city centrals or "trades' unions" were formed in a number of Eastern cities. In 1834, delegates from several of these created the first national labor organization in the United States, the National Trades' Union, the only one to this day to organize as a federation of city centrals. The dominant labor issue of the 1830's was the ten-hour day. Strikes for the ten-hour day were successful in the skilled trades of several cities, and a major objective of the National Trades' Union was to win the ten-hour day in federal government employment. This objective was achieved in 1840, when President Van Buren signed an executive order establishing the ten-hour day in government work without reduction in daily pay. However, the National Trades' Union did not survive to see its victory. Along with many local organizations, it had fallen victim to the severe depression that began in 1837.

In retrospect the decade of the 1840's represents a diversion of the American labor movement from its ultimate line of development. Much of the leadership of this period was furnished by intellectuals who had never been manual workers, and much of the energy of the movement went into the formation of co-operative societies, especially producers' co-operatives. Producers' co-operatives, which were again to become important after the Civil War, are workshops or factories owned by their workers. None was more than temporarily successful; most failed from bad management or lack of capital, and the few that did not eventually become ordinary private-profit companies by refusing to admit new employees into the ranks of owners.

In the early 1850's, the first permanent national unions were formed; the National Typographical Union is generally credited with being the oldest, followed shortly by the machinists, the molders, and the locomotive engineers. A national union was originally a federation of local unions in the same craft or trade in different localities. It was soon to become the most important level of union organization, and today it is in most cases more nearly correct to describe the local unions as subordinate bodies of national unions than to describe the national as a federation of locals. The development of national unions in the 1850's is related to the improvement in internal transportation and communication brought about by the growth of the railroad. In part, national unions arose in response to the problem of competition in product markets as goods made in low-wage areas were sold in the same markets as those made by local unions that had won higher wage scales. In other cases, national unions were formed to deal with problems raised by union members who moved from one city to another, sometimes in response to wage differentials, and sought admission to the union of their trade when they reached their destinations. Rules for the admission of itinerant members were an important part of the business of many early national unions.[1]

The growth of the labor movement was stimulated by the inflation of the Civil War and the resulting tight market for labor. New local and national unions were formed and existing unions gained members. In 1866 a new attempt was made to form a central federation of American labor, the National Labor Union. This loose organization of national unions, city centrals, and local unions lasted only six years. Initially, it gave its attention to the eight-hour day, an issue that was to concern the labor movement until the 1920's. Later it turned its energies increasingly to currency reform— the so-called greenback movement. Throughout the long decline in prices from 1865 to 1896, a period marked by two

[1] See Lloyd Ulman, *The Rise of the National Trade Union* (Cambridge, Mass.: Harvard University Press, 1955). Although we shall refer to national unions throughout this book, the official name of most of these organizations is now "international union" because they have some local unions in Canada. A staff member of such a union is often called an "international representative."

major depressions, the labor movement supported various "easy money" programs whose details need not concern us here. This position may have been taken in part in the hope of stimulating employment, but the more immediate objective was to protect working-class debtors from a rising real burden of debt created by falling prices.

By 1870, the national unions had become dissatisfied with the political program of the National Labor Union and their withdrawal from it speeded its decline. Increasingly the national unions were becoming the hard core of the labor movement. Several labor unions of this period were organized as secret societies to avoid employer reprisals against members, and many had various insurance or benefit features. The names of some of these unions suggest their close relation to lodges and fraternal orders: The Knights of St. Crispin (a large but short-lived union of shoemakers), and the Noble Order of the Knights of Labor. This fraternal flavor lingers in the union movement today in such things as the title of officers in some unions (for example, Grand Chief Engineer of the Brotherhood of Locomotive Engineers), in the use of the term "lodge" for locals in the machinists' union, and in the universally used complimentary opening and closing of letters "Dear Sir and Brother" and "Fraternally yours."

Like earlier severe depressions, that of the 1870's seriously weakened the trade unions. One estimate states that the number of national unions dropped from about thirty in 1873 to nine in 1877.[1] During 1877, the United States experienced its most extensive labor disputes up to that time—large-scale strikes of railroad workers against wage cuts. Railroad traffic was paralyzed in large sections of the country, and federal troops were used to restore order following riots in Pittsburgh, Baltimore, and other cities. The strikes were largely spontaneous, since as yet few railroad workers were organized; they ended in defeat for the workers, probably because the outbreak of violence turned public sentiment against them.

[1] Foster Rhea Dulles, *Labor in America* (New York: Thomas Y. Crowell Co., 1955), p. 112.

After 1877 there was a revival of business and a renewed growth of unions. The Knights of Labor, which had been founded in 1869 and had survived the depression of the 1870's as a secret society, came into the open in 1878 and grew rapidly in the early 1880's. Membership in the Knights was not restricted to skilled craftsmen, as was that of almost all earlier organizations. The unskilled were included, and in principle those who were not wage-earners at all—only lawyers, doctors, bankers, and dealers in liquor were originally barred from membership. Some affiliates of the Knights (the trade assemblies) were in effect local craft unions, but most were of mixed composition (district assemblies), cutting across lines of industry and trade. The organization was much more centralized than earlier national federations, and it emphasized political action and producer co-operation rather than the setting of wages and hours through negotiations with employers. In principle, the Knights opposed the use of strikes. However, their greatest success occurred when some of their district assemblies on the railroads won major strikes against wage cuts and the discriminatory firing of union members. The most spectacular victory was won in 1885, when the Wabash Railroad settled a strike by agreeing not to discriminate against members of the Knights. The Wabash was then controlled by Jay Gould, one of the most powerful financiers of the time. Following this victory, members flocked into the Knights, which reportedly reached a peak of 700,000 members in 1886.

The fall of the Knights of Labor was even more precipitous than its rise. There was a high turnover of membership and a critical lack of experienced leadership in the sprawling organization. In the second half of 1886, many important strikes were lost. The violent public reaction to the Haymarket riot of 1886 weakened support for unions and stiffened employer resistance.[1]   Neither the Knights nor the craft unions had any

[1] The Haymarket riot took place in Chicago on May 4, 1886, as an aftermath of a one-day demonstration strike for the eight-hour day. At a mass meeting called to protest the death of strikers killed in a

connection with the Haymarket riots. Nevertheless, they
were affected differently because the craft unions were better
prepared to withstand a period of adversity. Trade assemblies
of the Knights began to disaffiliate or to lose ground to older
unions, and the more diverse district assemblies lost members
rapidly.

By the early 1890's, the Knights had virtually disappeared.
Their disappearance marks a major turning point in American
labor history. Never again was a major labor organization
to put its main emphasis on legislation and producer co-
operation rather than on setting the wages, hours, and working
conditions of its own members. By 1890, the triumph of
business unionism was assured.

The growth of business unionism in the 1880's was also
marked by the formation of a new central federation of the
craft unions. Founded in 1881 as the Federation of Organized
Trades and Labor Unions, it was reorganized in 1886 as the
American Federation of Labor. Despite a brief threat to its
pre-eminence in the 1930's, it has remained the dominant
central federation of American labor ever since.

The leading figure in the new federation was Samuel
Gompers of the cigar-makers' union. Like many, if not most
of the craft unionists of this time, Gompers was an immigrant.
Although he had studied Marx as a young man, he had rejected
Socialist views in favor of a highly pragmatic philosophy.
The principles he laid down for the American Federation of
Labor (the AF of L) were to survive for more than forty years,
and Gompers was the president of that body in every year but

picket-line struggle, a bomb exploded among a detachment of police, killing
one policeman and injuring several. There were more deaths on both
sides in the fighting that followed. Eight members of a small but highly
vocal anarchist group were convicted of carrying out the bombing;
five were executed and three imprisoned. Governor John Peter Altgeld
of Illinois later concluded that there was no evidence connecting the
anarchists with the bombing, and pardoned the three surviving prisoners.

The demonstrations of May 1, 1886, in Chicago are the origin of May
Day, celebrated as a labor or radical holiday in most of the world except
the United States.

one from its founding to his death in 1925. His principles for the new federation were these: (1) every affiliated national union was to have complete autonomy in running its internal affairs; (2) each affiliate was to have an exclusive jurisdiction and no other affiliate was to organize workers in this jurisdiction; (3) the AF of L was to avoid any permanent commitment to support any political party, using its political influence instead to support its friends and punish its enemies, regardless of party lines; (4) the AF of L favored the improvement of wages, hours, and working conditions through the direct efforts of trade unions, and until the 1930's opposed efforts to improve the terms of employment through legislation. This last principle became known as the principle of voluntarism. The principles of the new federation were so appealing to the national unions that all those of any importance, except the brotherhoods of operating employees on the railroads, soon joined.

Among the unskilled workers who had attempted to organize in the period following the Civil War were the coal miners in both bituminous and anthracite coal fields. Until 1890, however, they had not succeeded in forming a permanent organization. In that year, the United Mine Workers was formed and became the first successful industrial union—a union that takes in all the wage-earners in an industry or group of related industries without regard to skill, craft, or occupation. The AF of L was later to recognize the right of the mine workers to organize such skilled workers as carpenters within its industry despite the jurisdictional claims of the carpenters union. During the late 1890's, the United Mine Workers won a firm footing in the northern bituminous coal fields from Pennsylvania west to Illinois, and reached agreement with the mine operators on wages and hours.

Other attempts to form industrial unions in the 1890's were less successful. The Amalgamated Association of Iron, Steel, and Tin Workers, which had achieved some success as a union of skilled workers in the steel industry, lost a crucial strike in 1892 at Homestead, Pennsylvania. The strike issue was union opposition to wage cuts. The employer, the Carnegie Steel Company, brought 300 armed guards from the Pinkerton Detective Agency to the mill by barge, and a gun battle was fought between the guards and the strikers, killing several on both sides. This led to intervention by state militia and the eventual defeat of the union. Thereafter, the Amalgamated was never again to achieve large-scale organization in the steel industry. It remained an unimportant union confined to a handful of skilled craftsmen until it was eventually absorbed in the Steel Workers' Organizing Committee late in the 1930's.

A second major union defeat took place in Chicago in 1894— the famous Pullman strike. The strike began as a struggle of workers in the Pullman car shops to restore a wage cut. These workers belonged to the American Railway Union, formed in 1893 as an industrial union of railway workers. Its leader, Eugene V. Debs, was a former official of the Brotherhood of Locomotive Firemen who had become convinced that craft unions on the railroads were less effective than one big union would be. He was later to become the leader of the Socialist party and its frequent candidate for President. Debs extended the strike to the railways when members of his union, in sympathy with the striking Pullman workers, refused to move Pullman sleeping cars. The strike brought to public attention the developing use of injunctions by federal courts in labor disputes. A federal district court enjoined any person from inducing railway workers to refuse to work, and Debs was eventually jailed for six months for contempt of court through disobedience to the injunction. The use of federal troops, sent by President Cleveland over the objections of Governor Altgeld of Illinois, also contributed to the collapse of the strike. The American Railway Union did not survive this defeat, and craft unionism remained almost the exclusive form of unionism in the railroads from this time on.

The American Federation of Labor and the major national unions weathered the depression of the 1890's better than unions had weathered any previous major depression.

Beginning in 1898 there was a rapid growth in union membership, especially in mining, the railroads, and the building
trades. Annual estimates of union membership are available
starting with 1897. Table 1 shows union membership at
selected dates, chosen so as to highlight the major trends in
union growth. The period of growth from 1897 to 1904 is
one of the most rapid on record. It coincided with vigorous
prosperity and economic growth that followed the depressed
conditions of the mid-1890's.

TABLE 1

REPORTED MEMBERSHIP OF NATIONAL AND INTERNATIONAL UNIONS,
SELECTED DATES, 1897–1958

Year	Thousands of Members[a]	Per Cent of Nonagricultural Employment[b]
1897	447	
1904	2,073	
1914	2,687	
1920	5,048	
1929	3,461	
1933	2,689	11.5
1937	7,001	22.8
1941	10,201	28.2
1945	14,322	35.8
1948	14,300[c]	32.2
1952	15,900[c]	32.9
1956	17,490	33.7
1958	16,786	33.2

Source: *Historical Statistics of the United States* (1960), pp. 97–98 and *Monthly Labor
Review* (January, 1960), pp. 1–9.

[a] Data for 1897–1929 include Canadian members of unions with headquarters in the
United States (Wolman's data). The estimated number of Canadian members included
is 255,000 in 1920 and 203,000 in 1930. Data for 1933–58 exclude Canadian members
(Bureau of Labor Statistics data).

[b] Number of members divided by employment in nonagricultural establishments; the
latter series excludes domestic servants and the self-employed.

[c] Rounded to the nearest hundred.

As the rapid growth in union membership slowed to a more
modest pace after 1904, dissatisfaction appeared in some parts
of the labor movement with the conservative policies of the
AF of L. In 1905 a convention was held that formed the
Industrial Workers of the World, the last important national

organization to challenge the philosophy of business unionism. The original convention of the IWW contained a wide assortment of dissident union leaders and other radicals. However, many of the original groups soon left the organization, and the remaining leaders developed a militant syndicalist philosophy, stressing the use of strikes and other forms of direct action to win the eventual abolition of the wage system and the replacement of existing forms of government by organizations of all workers along industrial lines. In the early years of the IWW, its strength was concentrated in the West, especially among lumberjacks and migrant workers. However, in 1912 and 1913 it conducted some very large and successful strikes among the woolen workers of Massachusetts and the silk workers of New Jersey. Like the Knights of Labor, however, the IWW proved unable to use these temporary victories as the basis of permanent organization. The IWW vigorously opposed United States participation in World War I. This position led to a rapid decline in its strength, assisted at times by mob violence against it and by newly passed laws against "criminal syndicalism." After the war the IWW became a tiny organization whose status as a labor union was questionable. A remnant survives to this day, with headquarters on North Halstead Street in Chicago.

The more conventional unions were also having difficulties with the law in the period just before World War I. In 1908, the Supreme Court upheld a judgment against the hatters' union of triple damages of more than half a million dollars in a suit brought under the terms of the Sherman Antitrust Act. This action resulted from a consumer boycott by the national union against a non-union producer of hats in Danbury, Connecticut. The Danbury Hatters' decision was based on the view that reducing the flow of goods in interstate commerce by a boycott was "restraint of trade" in the meaning of this antimonopoly act; in later decisions this same rather strained interpretation of the act was applied to strikes that limited the flow of goods in interstate commerce. This interpretation of the antitrust laws was not reversed until 1940, though as early as 1914 Congress had amended the laws in part in an effort to preclude this construction of them.[1]

A second legal device used to check the spread of union organization was the so-called "yellow-dog contract." This was a document signed by a worker stating that as a condition of employment he agreed not to join a union. Unions that attempted to organize workers who had signed such agreements were found guilty of inducing breach of contract. Several states and the federal government had passed laws making the yellow-dog contract illegal, but in 1917 the Supreme Court in the Hitchman case upheld a 1907 injunction against the United Mine Workers and found the laws prohibiting yellow-dog contracts unconstitutional.

Though legal obstacles may have slowed the growth of unions in the decade from 1904 to 1914, the tight labor markets during World War I helped to bring about a new spurt of rapid growth. This was assisted by temporary government guarantees of the right to organize undertaken in an effort to avert strikes that might interrupt war production. Even under these favorable conditions, the unions failed to organize some heavy industries. The most notable failure was in steel, where a major strike and organizing effort in 1919 was unsuccessful. However, industrial unions in the clothing industry, organized just before the war, prospered during the wartime boom and became successful permanent organizations. The peak of the rise in union membership was reached in the postwar inflation of 1920; the sharp recession of 1921 brought an end to the expansion.

From 1923 to 1929 the economy experienced a fortunate combination of prosperity and stable prices. The unions however, failed to benefit from these conditions. Instead of growing as in earlier prosperous periods, they gradually lost strength. In some cases the losses resulted from mistakes by the unions themselves. For example, the United Mine Workers, which had won a very high wage scale in the northern

[1] See Charles O. Gregory, *Labor and the Law* (New York: W. W. Norton Co., 1958), Chapters VIII and X.

bituminous coal industry, lost strength as production shifted rapidly to the non-union fields of the South. In most cases, however, employer policy was more important in the 1920's than union policy. Employers continued to resist unionization in most manufacturing industries, but to this historic negative resistance many began to add a new active concern for employee welfare and employee relations, and to set up special staffs of personnel administrators. One objective of this movement was to forestall unions by averting worker grievances. The one bright spot from the union point of view was the railroads. Here the unions and management jointly drafted the Railway Labor Act, which was enacted in 1926. This was the first permanent federal guarantee of the right to bargain collectively. It also established special federal machinery for resolving labor disputes in the railroad industry.

The Great Depression that began in 1929 was at first a very severe blow to the unions. Reported membership fell by almost a fifth in four years. The statistics undoubtedly understate the extent of the decline. Many unions continued to carry unemployed members on the rolls, although they were not charged dues, and others were simply unwilling to report their true weakness. Most unions were forced to accept wage cuts and in many cases the fall in actual wages was greater than the reduction in the announced union scale.

At the depths of the depression, however, changes took place in legislation and in public attitudes toward unions that were to usher in a new period of rapid union growth. The first of these was the adoption of the Norris-LaGuardia Act in 1932.[1] This law severely restricted the right of federal courts to issue injunctions in labor disputes and made yellow-dog contracts

[1] All of the important federal laws governing labor relations with the exception of the Railway Labor Act are commonly known by the names of their principal Congressional sponsors and these names will be used in the text throughout the book. Thus the National Labor Relations Act of 1935 will be called the Wagner Act, the Labor-Management Relations Act of 1948 will be called the Taft-Hartley Act, and the Labor-Management Reporting and Disclosure Act of 1959 will be called the Landrum-Griffin Act.

unenforcible in federal courts. Later in the same year the election of Franklin D. Roosevelt marked the beginning of a period of strong support for organized labor by the federal government. In 1933, the National Industrial Recovery Act was passed; it included a provision (section 7a) that employees should have the right to bargain collectively through representatives of their own choosing. This provision led to a new burst of organizing activity by the unions, expressed first when older unions in such areas as coal mining and clothing began to win back their control of their jurisdictions. In many industries, however, employers responded to the new law by organizing employee representation plans, free of influence from "outside" unions and severely limited in their powers to make demands on the employer.

Early in 1935, the National Industrial Recovery Act was found unconstitutional by the Supreme Court. However, a substitute for its labor provisions was quickly enacted. Indeed, the Wagner Act of 1935 went well beyond the old law, for it made it an unfair labor practice for a company to encourage or support a labor organization, thus banning the employee representation plans organized under the NIRA. In addition the law made it an unfair labor practice for employers to discriminate against union members and provided machinery (the National Labor Relation Board) for hearing complaints against employers of unfair labor practices and for conducting representation elections among workers to determine their bargaining representative. Board orders could be appealed to the courts and if they were upheld, noncompliance could be punished as contempt. The act covered all workers whose work affected interstate commerce except those covered by the Railway Labor Act, which had been broadened to include air transportation. Employers were generally opposed to the Wagner Act, and many large corporations ignored its provisions until 1937 when its constitutionality was upheld by the Supreme Court in the Jones and Laughlin case.

Under the provisions of the NIRA and the Wagner Act, union membership more than doubled in the years from 1933 to 1937.

This rapid growth was accompanied by conflict within the union movement and by several major industrial disputes. The internal conflict began when workers in the automobile and rubber industries, encouraged by the new legislation, began to form local industrial unions. These unions applied for admission to the AF of L and were given so-called federal charters—that is, they were affiliated directly with the AF of L itself rather than with one of the existing national unions. The new federal locals wanted to form national industrial unions in their industries. However, the craft unions in the AF of L wanted the charters of the proposed national unions to exclude craft workers in the occupational jurisdictions of the older unions. This proposal was unacceptable both to the new unions and to the older industrial unions in the AF of L, of which the United Mine Workers, the Amalgamated Clothing Workers, and the International Ladies' Garment Workers were the most important. At the 1935 convention of the AF of L, the issue could not be compromised, and the craft unions won the day by a substantial majority. The industrial unions, led by John L. Lewis of the United Mine Workers, formed the Committee for Industrial Organization. This was originally intended as a committee within the AF of L but was quickly branded a "dual organization" by the AF of L executive council and ordered to disband. When it refused to do so, its member unions were expelled from the AF of L. In 1938 the new group changed its name to Congress of Industrial Organizations (CIO) and until 1955 functioned as a separate and rival federation.

The new national industrial unions in the auto and rubber industries received assistance from the older CIO unions and were soon ready to demand recognition from employers. When this was not willingly granted, the unions developed a new form of strike, the sit-down strike. The striking workers continued to occupy the struck factories, and food was furnished to them by supporters on the outside. Although this technique was later to be held illegal by the courts, it gained a foothold for the unions in the automobile and rubber industries. State authorities hesitated to eject the strikers by force or to starve them into submission, since such a plan might have caused many deaths among the unarmed strikers. The greatest victory for the sit-down strikers came in early 1937, when the General Motors Corporation recognized the United Automobile Workers as bargaining agent for its members employed by General Motors.

In the meanwhile, the CIO had also been conducting a successful organizing drive in the basic steel industry through a new organization called the Steel Workers' Organizing Committee (SWOC), later to become the United Steelworkers of America. This group was supplied with funds and skilled leaders by the United Mine Workers and operated in part by working within the employee representation plans which had been widely organized in the steel industry. When the management of the United States Steel Corporation became convinced that the leaders of the employee representation plans had swung over to the new union, it decided to avert a strike for recognition. In March, 1937, United States Steel voluntarily recognized the SWOC as the bargaining agent for its members and granted a wage increase in an agreement negotiated for the union by John L. Lewis. Other companies in the industry were not to yield so readily. Attempts to organize the other major producers led to a bitter strike at several companies, marked by outbursts of violence. On May 30, 1937, ten strikers were killed by police gunfire at the South Chicago plant of Republic Steel, an incident known to the unions as the "Memorial Day Massacre." The SWOC lost the "little steel strike" and the companies involved did not recognize the union until they were ordered to do so by the War Labor Board in 1941.

The formation of the CIO spurred the older unions of the AF of L to new and vigorous organizing efforts, and the AF of L soon recouped the losses in total membership caused by the withdrawal of the CIO unions. In the process of competition, the neat distinction between craft and industrial unions became blurred. Thus the AF of L Amalgamated

Meat Cutters and Butcher Workmen, a craft union in retail
food stores, became an industrial union in the meat-packing
industry in competition with the CIO United Packinghouse
Workers of America; the AF of L International Association
of Machinists, a craft union in the railroads and some other
industries, became an industrial union in the growing aircraft
industry in competition with the CIO auto workers.

World War II brought further growth in union membership.
The unions gave a no-strike pledge to prevent interference with
war production.   In return, they received assistance from the
War Labor Board in winning recognition from employers who
had not previously granted it, and in establishing stable
collective bargaining relationships with these employers.
The board was a tripartite body representing unions, management, and the public established to settle wartime labor
disputes and to control wage rates.   In addition to winning
new members by extending their sphere of organization, the
unions also gained from the rapid expansion of employment
where they were already established as war production
absorbed the unemployed and drew new workers into the
labor force.

The war period led to serious ideological conflict within the
CIO unions.   Members of the Communist party had been
active in several of these unions in their early days and had
proved themselves skilful and dedicated organizers.   In the
war years, their political program began to diverge from union
purposes.   Before the German attack on the Soviet Union in
June, 1941, the Communists were strongly opposed to the
war and were accused by non-Communists leaders of instigating
strikes in defense plants to obstruct American aid to the Allies.
After June, 1941, the Communist leaders suddenly became
more willing than their opponents to sacrifice union objectives
for increased production.   Bitter factional disputes took place
for the control of several CIO unions.   In some unions,
notably the United Automobile Workers, the non-Communists
eventually achieved complete victory.   In others, however,
Communists and their sympathizers gained control.

In 1948 the CIO expelled several unions on charges of Communist domination. Some of these expelled unions are still in existence, including the United Electrical Workers, which claimed 160,000 members in 1958, and the Mine, Mill, and Smelter Workers which claimed 100,000 members. The International Longshoremen's and Warehousemen's Union still represents longshoremen on the Pacific Coast. Unlike such earlier left-wing unions as the Industrial Workers of the World, the unions of this group do not differ appreciably in their day-to-day operation from other contemporary national unions. Far from proclaiming a Communist philosophy, they deny that they are under Communist control.

The expulsion of the left-wing unions from the CIO and the earlier withdrawal of some of its other affiliates left the organization considerably smaller than the AF of L. The United Mine Workers had withdrawn in 1940, when the CIO supported the re-election of Franklin D. Roosevelt despite John L. Lewis' support of Wendell Willkie. The two leading unions in the postwar CIO were the United Automobile Workers and the United Steelworkers, and increasingly the presidents of these large unions were unfriendly rivals. At the same time, the original differences between the CIO and the AF of L were rapidly diminishing, for the AF of L in practice had not effectively protected the jurisdiction of craft unions against industrial organization by its own affiliates. Most of the men who had been the leading participants in the bitter rivalries of the 1930's had died or retired, or their unions were not in either federation. In 1955 the two federations reunited and established the American Federation of Labor and Congress of Industrial Organizations (AFL–CIO) as the new sole central federation of American labor. However, some jurisdictional conflict between craft and industrial unions continued within the new merged federation.

The public attitude toward unions in the postwar period was less favorable than it had been in the 1930's, and this attitude was soon expressed in a move toward greater government neutrality. The Taft-Hartley Act of 1948 made a large number of detailed changes in the Wagner Act, many of them designed to restore rights to employers or individual workers. For example, unions as well as employers could now be found guilty of unfair labor practices, and elections could be held to decertify unions as bargaining agents as well as to certify them. Although organized labor denounced the law as a "slave labor law," its strenuous efforts to achieve repeal or major changes have been unsuccessful. The Taft-Hartley Act did not materially reduce union strength where unions were already well established, though it has contributed to the slower extension of unionism to new territory in the postwar period.

Congressional investigations of unions in the late 1950's disclosed a number of instances of corruption and misuse of union funds. In response to these disclosures, the AFL–CIO established an ethical practices committee which investigated several affiliated national unions. When some of these unions refused to clean house, they were expelled from the federation. However, in some cases expulsion did not appreciably weaken them; the largest, the International Brotherhood of Teamsters, continued to thrive. In 1959 Congress passed the Landrum-Griffin Act in an attempt to police internal union affairs. Among other provisions, the act required complete public disclosure of union finances and required the regular holding of conventions and elections. The problem of corruption in unions is discussed further in Chapter XI.

Union growth in the postwar period has been largely due to growth in the size of the labor force. As a percentage of non-agricultural employment, union membership has remained quite stable in the neighborhood of one-third. The membership data for several postwar years are given in Table 1.

§ 3. The Present Extent of Union Organization. As of 1958, the membership of national unions in the United States was estimated at 16.8 million. The same unions had another 1.2 million members in Canada. In addition, independent local unions had a reported membership of 700,000 as of 1956, and this figure is undoubtedly too low because of incomplete reporting. The full number has been estimated at roughly 1,500,000.[1]

Of the 186 national unions reporting in 1958 to the Bureau of Labor Statistics, 137 were affiliated with the AFL–CIO. These affiliates had a membership of 13.9 million in the United States, while the 49 independent national unions had a U.S. membership of 2.9 million.

The membership reported by the ten largest national unions is shown in Table 2. In some cases, these unions may include unemployed or retired members in their reported membership. Thus the United Mine Workers reported 600,000 members in 1958, although production worker employment in coal mining in that year averaged less than 200,000 and it seems improbable that the Mine Workers had more than 100,000 employed members in other industries. At the other end of the size scale, there were 89 national unions reporting fewer than 25,000 members each in 1958, and of these 14 had fewer than 1,000 members. These smallest national unions are largely craft unions in unusual or moribund crafts.

The extent of union organization differs greatly in different sectors of the economy. In construction, coal and metal mining, and transportation and public utilities the great majority of wage-earners are union members. A large majority of manufacturing wage-earners are union members, though there are parts of manufacturing, especially textiles, where only a minority of workers are organized. These four sectors—manufacturing, construction, mining, and transportation and public utilities—account for more than 80 per cent of union membership, and manufacturing alone accounts for almost half. In the service and distributive industries, unionism is generally weak, though among certain skilled

[1] Additional information on independent local unions is given in two articles by Leo Troy: "Local Independent and National Unions: Competitive Labor Organizations," *Journal of Political Economy*, October, 1960, and "Local Independent Unions and the American Labor Movement, *Industrial and Labor Relations Review*, April, 1961.

TABLE 2

REPORTED MEMBERSHIP OF THE TEN LARGEST
NATIONAL UNIONS, 1958

International Brotherhood of Teamsters[a]	1,418,446
United Automobile Workers	1,027,000
International Association of Machinists	992,689
United Steelworkers of America	960,000
Brotherhood of Carpenters and Joiners	835,000
International Brotherhood of Electric Workers . . .	750,000
United Mine Workers[a]	600,000
Hod Carriers and Common Laborers	476,598
International Ladies' Garment Workers' Union . .	442,901
Hotel and Restaurant Workers	436,315

Source: *Monthly Labor Review*, January 1960.

[a] Independent. All other unions shown are affiliated with the AFL–CIO.

workers, such as musicians, bartenders, barbers, and meat-cutters, it is strong in most large cities.

There is also considerable geographic variation in the extent of union organization. Leo Troy's estimates by states for 1953 range from 53 per cent of non-agricultural employment in Washington to 8.3 per cent in North Carolina.[1] The estimates for most northern and western industrial states exceed one-third; those for most southern states are below one-fifth. There is an obvious interrelation between these estimates and those by industry, since the relative importance of industries in non-agricultural employment differs from state to state.

National unions have more than two million clerical and professional workers among their membership, and a few unions of clerical workers, such as the Brotherhood of Railway Clerks, have achieved considerable size and strength. On the whole, however, white-collar workers have been slow to join unions, and the strength of the union movement has been primarily among craftsmen, operatives, and laborers.

[1] Leo Troy, *Distribution of Union Membership Among the States, 1939 and 1953*, "Occasional Paper" 56; National Bureau of Economic Research, 1957.

The number of women members in national unions is estimated at 3.3 million in 1958. Of these, about 20 per cent were in apparel industries. Women make up about 18 per cent of the membership of national unions, though they constitute more than 30 per cent of the labor force.

The extent of union organization of the non-agricultural labor force depends both on the success with which unions organize particular occupations and industries and on the nature of shifts in the industrial and occupational composition of employment. Between 1947 and 1960 there was an absolute decline in the number of workers in the most heavily unionized sectors of the economy. Total employment declined in mining and in transportation and public utilities, and production worker employment declined in manufacturing. Only in contract construction among the heavily unionized sectors did employment increase, and this increase did not fully offset the declines in the other three areas. The recent stability of union membership relative to the non-agricultural labor force can thus be viewed as the outcome of two opposing tendencies: an increasing extent of unionization within given sectors of the economy, offset by a decline on the relative importance of the sectors in which union strength is greatest, and especially in the fraction of the total labor force consisting of manual workers. Current changes in technology seem likely to reduce further the proportion of manual workers in the labor force. Future gains in the extent of unionization will depend largely on the ability of unions to organize professional, clerical, and sales workers on a larger scale than in the past.

§ 4. **The Structure of Unions.** The diversity of unions has invited social taxonomists to distinguish and name a wide variety of types. The classification used here is a minimal one, intended to distinguish only the types important in subsequent discussion. As we have seen, the crucial distinction is that between the craft union and the industrial union. The craft union includes workers in the same occupation or craft or group of related crafts. The craft may be confined to one industry (locomotive engineers, for example) or may spread across many (electricians, machinists). In contrast, the industrial union organizes all the wage-earners in a given industry or group of related industries, regardless of occupation. The industrial union thus includes both skilled and semiskilled or unskilled workers. The craft union is generally an organization of the skilled. However, where the skilled workers in an industry have been organized by craft unions, an organization of those remaining becomes in effect a craft union of the unskilled, like the Hod Carriers and Common Laborers in the construction industry.

The central federation of American unions, the AFL–CIO, does not engage in collective bargaining—this is done by the national unions and their subordinate bodies. It acts as the principal spokesman of unions to the federal government and to foreign union movements, and as a research, educational, and public relations organization. It plays some role in the organization of new unions, and in recent years has formulated standards of ethical conduct for its member unions. State and local federations of local unions of AFL–CIO affiliates perform analagous political and public relations functions within their jurisdictions.

The principal locus of political and economic power in the American union movement has long been the national unions. The power of the AFL–CIO over its member national unions is limited by the ability of the larger nationals to function successfully outside it. The secession or expulsion of a large national union often hurts the AFL–CIO more than it hurts the national union.

Almost all national unions have subordinate local unions, through which the individual member participates in union affairs. In industries where the individual plant or establishment is large, the members of a local industrial union are usually all workers in the same establishment. In most craft unions, the local has a geographical jurisdiction—the members of a craft in a given city or county. The craft basis of a local is often finer than that of its national union. Thus the bricklayers, masons, and plasterers, members of the same national union, have separate locals in most cities.

Where the product market is local, as in the building trades and the service industries, the local union usually has great independence in bargaining. In industries with national product markets, the economic terms of bargaining are generally set by the national union, and local union activity is concentrated on the functions of administering the agreement. In some unions, bodies intermediate between the local and the national have become important in economic bargaining. In the over-the-road trucking industry, for example, regional conferences of the teamsters' union have become very powerful union bodies. In other unions, geographical districts are important units through which the national union provides services to the locals.

In addition to the national unions and their locals, there are many independent local unions representing the workers of a single plant or company. These are often successors to the company-dominated or -supported unions of the 1930's. However, company domination or support of unions has now been illegal for more than twenty years, and the independent local unions of today are independent both of the company and of the rest of the union movement. In some industries, notably chemicals, petroleum refining, and telephone, they form an important part of total union membership. Elsewhere, they are more widely scattered, often as enclaves in an industry organized by a national union. Such a position can be an advantageous one—the members of the independent local union may receive all the economic gains won by the national union, and in addition work steadily while the national union is on strike. Independent local unions also appeal to some professional workers, such as engineers, who are reluctant to identify themselves with unions of wage-earners.

The structure of American unionism is not a neat, planned structure, but one that has evolved from a long process of political and economic struggle. Some rivalries between unions, like that between the brewery workers and the teamsters over who shall represent the drivers of beer trucks, have been going on for sixty or seventy years and can still erupt from time to time.   Most national unions include some anomalous locals, especially in the geographical areas of their greatest strength. Thus in Chicago, a local union of retail clerks is affiliated with the national union of building service workers and at least three other national unions represent other groups of retail clerks. But it is unimportant whether such arrangements seem neat to the outside observer so long as they seem fitting to the workers concerned.

§ **5. Why Workers Join Unions.**   The historical record seems to suggest that American workers form and join unions largely to win higher wages and shorter hours.   Contemporary investigation reveals a more complex set of motives.   In part, the difference lies in the fact that for a worker employed in an already unionized establishment, wages and hours are the same whether he is a union member or not.   Thus it may require additional motives or pressures to lead him to join and to pay union dues.

The relative importance of the desire to help in maintaining union wage scales as a motive for supporting the union may be greatest in some of the craft unions.   Even here, however, other motives are also present.   Where workers work in scattered and shifting locations, the local union serves as an important meeting place for friends who have at times past worked on the same job.   The benefit features of many craft unions also remain influential in winning support.

In industrial unions, many workers join because of some incident in the plant in which they experienced or witnessed what they considered to be unfair or arbitrary action by a foreman or supervisor.   The possibility of limiting or redressing such action through the grievance procedure is thus a primary motive for union membership and support of the organization.   In a study of a large local industrial union in which 114 leaders, active members, and rank and file members were interviewed about their reasons for joining the union, such experiences were frequently mentioned, though not one worker mentioned wages.[1]

Other important factors revealed in the same study that influenced the decision to join this industrial union were a background of union or radical activity in the worker's family or childhood, or previous membership or activity in another union. Workers who did not have a reason for joining in terms of family background or experience in the plant often reported that they joined largely because it was the normal thing to do in this plant—because almost everyone else was a member. Where this general pressure for conformity with the environment failed to persuade the reluctant worker, more direct persuasion or social pressure was often applied.

Increasingly, the decision to join the union is not a voluntary one; membership is often required as a condition of employment under the terms of closed shop or union shop contract. Such contracts will be considered further in Chapter VI. The prevalence of contracts that require union membership should not be interpreted to mean that most union members have joined against their will. When worker approval of the union shop was required through government-conducted elections in the early years of the Taft-Hartley Act, the great majority of all votes cast in such elections favored the union shop.

§ 6. Collective Bargaining. This section will be concerned only with the mechanics of collective bargaining. The substance will be considered in later chapters.

Collective bargaining is the process by which unions deal with employers to arrive at and administer agreements governing the terms of employment. The first step in this process is for the union to win recognition as the bargaining agent representing a group of employees. Before 1935, such recognition was either granted voluntarily by the employer or was won by the union through a strike. Since the passage of

[1] Joel Seidman, Jack London, and Bernard Karsh, "Why Workers Join Unions," *The Annals of the American Academy of Political and Social Science*, March, 1951.

the Wagner Act and its approval by the Supreme Court, these
methods have been used less frequently, though they are still
used where the channels provided by law seem too slow.
Typically, however, recognition is now granted when a union
wins an election conducted by the National Labor Relations
Board in which employees choose a bargaining agent.

The Wagner Act and its successors guarantee workers the
right to organize and to bargain collectively in employments
affecting interstate commerce, an area which has been interpreted very broadly. Some industrial states guarantee similar
rights in intrastate employment. The NLRB holds elections
between rival unions or between a given union and no union,
and the employer is required to recognize a union that wins
such an election. The outcome of the election can depend
critically on how the bargaining unit is defined—that is, on
what group of workers is eligible to vote. In determining
rights, the board in general follows the historic lines of
bargaining in an industry, choosing craft units where these are
traditional and industrial units elsewhere. Since the passage
of the Taft-Hartley law, a group of skilled craftsmen within an
industrial plant is sometimes made a separate bargaining unit,
in which a craft union may win bargaining rights. A bargaining unit often includes more than one employer, especially in
craft groups where each employer has few employees and
turnover of workers and employers is high.

A union chosen as bargaining agent has an obligation to
represent all the employees in the bargaining unit, and not
merely its members. A defeated union can petition for a new
election after the passage of a suitable period of time. In the
meantime, it has no bargaining rights.

The exact nature of the employer's obligation to bargain is a
complicated legal question. In general, he must meet with the
representatives of the union and must put any agreement
reached into writing. He is not required by law to make
economic concessions but must go beyond merely saying no
to all union proposals.

The group of workers covered by one set of negotiations is

often larger than the bargaining unit in which elections are held. A national union whose locals have won the right to represent several plants of one employer will often negotiate a master contract covering all plants. In many industries, bargaining is conducted between a national or local union and an association representing many employers who deal with this union.

Increasingly, the collective agreement has tended to become a long and complicated document, and the parties to bargaining need the services of lawyers and specialists to help in specifying its terms. It is also becoming common for the agreement to run for a term of more than one year. Two, three, and even five year terms are not infrequent. In such cases it is even clearer than usual that collective bargaining goes beyond the process of reaching an agreement and includes the ways of interpreting the agreement and solving the problems that arise during its term.

Except during severe depressions, the union is usually the "aggressor" in collective bargaining, in the sense that management is reasonably content with the *status quo*, while the union seeks changes favorable to its members. However, there has been an increasing tendency in recent years for management to go beyond accepting or rejecting union demands, and to come into negotiations with a program of its own.

Many factors influence the outcome of collective bargaining, including the values and ethical standards of the parties as influenced by the history of the bargaining relationship and the climate of public opinion. At heart, however, the bargaining relationship is a power relationship, and when differences of view develop, their outcome depends ultimately on the ability of the parties to force concessions. In Chapter II we shall examine the sources of union power in collective bargaining.

CHAPTER II

THE SOURCES OF UNION POWER

§ 1. The Strike.   The strike is by far the most important source of union power, and the union is now virtually the sole organizer of strikes.   This last was not always true; at one time spontaneous strikes among unorganized workers were frequent.   In 1958, however, strikes that did not involve any union were less than 1 per cent of recorded strikes, and accounted for less than 0.05 per cent of man-days lost from strikes.[1]   Some unauthorized strikes of union members are still immediate expressions of worker discontent, but collective bargaining provides other channels for handling most grievances.

The strike is a planned withholding of labor designed to impose union demands on the employer or to prevent the employer from imposing his demands on the union.   It is traditional to divide work stoppages into strikes and lockouts, the former occurring where the workers walk off the job, the latter where the employer withholds employment from them.   But the employer almost never needs to do this.   At the expiration of an agreement he can always announce his terms unilaterally and allow the union the choices of striking, reaching an agreement, or working without an agreement during further negotiations.   Almost the only occasion for a true lockout arises when a union calls a strike against one member of an employers' association; the other employers

[1] U. S. Bureau of Labor Statistics, Bulletin No. 1258.   This is also the principal source of the other statistics in this section.

may then close down to make common cause with the struck employer. In this book, I shall use the word "strike" to cover all work stoppages, including the few that fit the traditional definition of the lockout.

The strike is the most conspicuous and dramatic aspect of labor relations and provides the labor movement with its heroes, martyrs, and folklore. To the general public, the prevention of strikes seems to be the chief problem in industrial relations and industrial peace is considered the chief goal. The economist is likely to be somewhat less concerned with the direct losses from strikes, and more concerned with the consequences as expressed in the terms of settlement. The strike keeps resources idle for days or months, but the settlement can determine the way in which resources are used for many years.

In recent years there have been roughly 3,000 to 5,000 recorded strikes a year in the United States (see Table 3). In 1958, a relatively peaceful year, there were 3,694 recorded strikes involving over 2 million workers and almost 24 million man-days of idleness. But this idleness was only 0.22 per cent of the estimated working time of all workers. The range of such estimates for 1947–60 is 0.14 to 0.61, and 1946 is the only year in which the estimated loss exceeded 1 per cent.

The available statistics are of limited value in assessing the cost of strikes. On the one hand, strikes also cause secondary idleness not included in the statistics. For example, a steel strike can cause railroad workers to be laid off for lack of traffic or automobile workers to be laid off for lack of materials. On the other hand, there are very important offsets to strike losses. Most strikes cause production to be displaced in time or location rather than to be lost altogether. A strike against one producer in a large industry may be completely offset by the increased output of his competitors. When an entire industry faces a threat of strike, it will often increase its output in anticipation; if the strike occurs, it may again produce at higher than normal levels for some time after the strike is over. If the industry struck is a supplier of materials to other industries, these industries can draw on inventories during the

TABLE 3

NUMBER OF STRIKES, WORKERS INVOLVED, AND
MAN-DAYS IDLE, 1946–60

YEAR	NUMBER OF STRIKES BEGINNING IN YEAR	WORKERS INVOLVED (1,000)	MAN-DAYS IDLE Number (1,000)	MAN-DAYS IDLE Per cent of estimated working time
1946	4,985	4,600	116,000	1.43
1947	3,693	2,170	34,600	0.41
1948	3,419	1,960	34,100	0.37
1949	3,606	3,030	50,500	0.59
1950	4,843	2,410	38,800	0.44
1951	4,737	2,220	22,900	0.23
1952	5,117	3,540	59,100	0.57
1953	5,091	2,400	28,300	0.26
1954	3,468	1,530	22,600	0.21
1955	4,320	2,650	28,200	0.26
1956	3,825	1,900	33,100	0.29
1957	3,673	1,390	16,500	0.14
1958	3,694	2,060	23,900	0.22
1959	3,708	1,880	69,000	0.61
1960	3,250	1,375	19,250	0.17

Source: *Historical Statistics of the United States*, 1960, p. 99, and Bulletins of the Bureau of Labor Statistics.

strike and replenish them afterward, so that there may be little effect on the output of final products.[1]

The possibility of offsets in time depends, of course, on the durability of the product. They are not possible for highly perishable goods or for services, and for many services offsets in location are also impossible. Since America has a large stock of automobiles and abundant facilities for keeping them in repair, a strike against automobile manufacturers could go on for months with little inconvenience to consumers. In contrast, a strike against a local bus line has an immediate impact. Moreover, if a bus strike prevents people from getting to work today, they will not be compensated by the possibility of going back and forth twice tomorrow. However, unions

[1] For an excellent analysis of the costs of steel strikes in terms of production of final products, see E. Robert Livernash, *Collective Bargaining in the Basic Steel Industry* (Washington, D.C.: U.S. Department of Labor, 1961), Chapter III.

and management go to great lengths to avoid strikes that would cause severe hardships to the public, and strikes that create real emergencies are fortunately rare.

In considering the costs of strikes, some non-economic factors should also be taken into account. A strike can have a cathartic effect, cleansing away accumulated tensions and making possible new approaches to stubborn problems. It can provide a release from the monotony of routine work and a sense of excitement not present in a mere vacation. Frequently such factors improve productivity when the strike is over. Of course, the costs of a prolonged strike can more than offset gains of this kind.

It is a favorite calculation of newspapers to compute the wage increases won in a strike and compare them with the wages lost during it, a calculation which often shows that workers have lost more wages than they will regain during the life of the agreement. Such calculations misjudge what is at stake. The strike is part of a long-range strategy for both parties. Union gains won without a strike are usually won through the threat of a strike, stated or implied. Such threats cannot retain much force if they are never carried out. Then too, in attempting to push gains just to the point at which a strike is averted, a union will sometimes misjudge its opponent. Once a strike is begun, whether through design or miscalculation, its settlement is not wholly a rational matter, but one that involves subtle questions of organizational and personal prestige. Union members can easily come to believe that the continued existence of their union is at stake, and they will then no longer reckon the outcome in cents per hour. It is no more possible to understand the causes or consequences of a strike by setting up a balance sheet than it would be for a dispute between nations.

Until about 1940, it was common for employers to attempt to operate struck plants, using non-striking employees or new employees recruited for the purpose. Unions engaged in mass picketing to prevent the strikebreakers or "scabs" from entering the plant. As we have seen in Chapter I, violence often occurred in such circumstances—fighting on the picket line, cars overturned, windows broken, and even shooting and dynamiting. The unions tended to be blamed for violence, though there were undoubtedly cases in which strikebreakers or employers were at fault. The outcome of such a strike depended critically on the position of the police and the courts. Injunctions against picketing and ample police protection for non-strikers could break the strike, and usually did. In a few more recent cases, police have prevented violence by forbidding strikebreakers to cross picket lines, an action that forces the employer to discontinue operations. Often the police or the courts now take a more lenient attitude toward strike violence than toward violence under most other circumstances.

Since World War II it has been unusual for employers to attempt to operate during a strike. The old pattern occurs largely in small communities and in the South. The effects of a strike where operations continue are particularly bitter in a small community. Friendships, social organizations, even families shatter as the community divides into strikers and strikebreakers, and the wounds may take years to heal.

Where the employer does not try to operate, the strike becomes a war of attrition. Around the silent factory, a few token pickets may chat with a lone policeman while their neatly painted signs lean against a fence. Maintenance crews may enter by prearrangement to keep equipment in good shape; sometimes the employer furnishes coffee and doughnuts to the pickets.

An effective strike imposes on both parties losses whose nature depends in large part on the scope of the strike. The employer must continue to meet fixed charges while receiving no revenues. If only one employer is struck in an industry, he may lose both customers and workers to competitors and he is not assured of getting all of them back when the strike ends. Customers often turn to more dependable suppliers or decide to produce their own requirements. At the same time, those strikers who cannot find other work are losing their wages. In some cases the union provides regular strike benefits, but these are possible chiefly in small strikes conducted by large unions.

The union strategy of striking one employer at a time, thus putting the struck employer at a competitive disadvantage, can be met by the formation of a united front among employers. This will usually force the union to strike a whole industry at once. If any competitive forces pressing employers toward settlement remain, they arise from other industries or from imports, and these pressures are usually weak. The dues of working union members cannot, in an industry-wide strike, provide benefits for the strikers. Benefits taken from accumulated strike funds or contributions from other unions will usually be reserved for cases of severe hardship. The ability of strikers to find work elsewhere will be sharply restricted. However, a strike against a whole industry can cause secondary unemployment on a large scale, or halt the flow of final products to consumers. The pressure of public opinion or the intervention of government may then force a settlement.

The ability of a union to win a strike depends on a number of factors. These are related to but not identical with the factors determining its ability to raise wages, which will be discussed in Chapter IV. A union can be said to win a strike when it gains concessions that the employers were unwilling to make before the strike, and when these meet, in whole or in large part, the union's true demands (as distinguished from demands made for tactical purposes).

A strike hurts an employer most if the demand for his product is strong and profits are high. If demand is weak, he may lose little by shutting down, and can more easily regain lost production when the strike is over. Perhaps in part for this reason, chronically depressed industries like apparel have had low strike rates. Similar forces produced a high correlation between the number of strikes and the level of business activity for the period 1915–1938.

Another major determinant of the union's ability to win is

the degree of skill and specialization of the members. The more skilled and specialized they are, the more difficult it is for management to carry on production by using strikebreakers or non-striking supervisory employees.

The ability of unions to win strikes does not necessarily govern the frequency with which they strike. If their power is great, mere threat of a strike may be all that is necessary. The propensity of a union to strike also depends in part on the philosophy and attitudes of its leaders and members. A high propensity to strike by unions of miners, seamen, and long-shoremen has been noted for several countries. A well-known study of this phenomenon suggests that the isolation of miners and maritime workers from the larger society contributes to this high propensity,[1] though this interpretation has been disputed by other scholars.

§ 2. **Government Intervention in Strikes.**   When a strike inflicts serious damage on neutral parties or on the general public, government is sooner or later forced to intervene. The party to the strike that considers itself least likely to win in the absence of intervention will encourage intervention by its statements or its behavior, while the other party will of course discourage it. The outcome of the strike will almost always be influenced by any forceful government intervention; only by the sheerest accident could strong intervention produce the result that would have occurred without it.

The intervention of government in many major strikes is an important reason why unions seek to develop political power even where they have little or no political program. The power to influence elections is a valuable adjunct to the power to strike. The role of government in strikes may also help to explain why American unions have largely avoided formal alliances with political parties. The more an elected official can be certain of the support of one party to an industrial

[1] See Clark Kerr and Abraham Siegel, "The Interindustry Propensity To Strike," in A. Kornhauser, R. Dubin, and A. Ross (eds.), *Industrial Conflict* (New York: McGraw-Hill Book Co., 1954).

dispute come what may, the more he may lean toward the other in an attempt to gain added political strength. Thus we observe, ironically, conspicuous instances of intervention favorable to unions by conservative elected officials, and of adverse intervention by officials with labor support.

There are many possible methods of government intervention in strikes, and it is not possible here to do more than mention a few. In arbitration, a neutral person or agency is appointed to settle the dispute, and his findings are binding upon the parties.[1] Because arbitrators tend to "split the difference" between the parties, the expectation that there will be arbitration encourages the parties to take and maintain extreme positions, and sharply reduces the chances of voluntary settlement. Systems of arbitration tend therefore to drift toward the widespread setting of the terms of employment by government bodies.

A second drawback of the arbitration of disputes over new agreements is the lack of any generally accepted standards of an equitable settlement. In wage disputes, arbitrators lean heavily on comparisons with wages elsewhere, but there is much room for disagreement about which comparisons are appropriate. A criterion that recommends itself to many economists is seldom applied, in part because arbitrators are more concerned with justice than with efficiency. This is the labor market criterion, which would call for wage increases if employers find it difficult to recruit suitable workers, and for no increases when many qualified workers are unemployed.

There are several methods of government intervention that fall short of arbitration, of which the most frequent is mediation (often called conciliation). The mediator tries to help the parties clarify their positions, resume negotiations if they have broken down, and formulate new compromises. In the words of one well-known mediator, "the essential function of the mediator is to keep the parties in intelligent discussion with

[1] This discussion does not apply to arbitration of disputes arising from the interpretation of existing agreements.

each other."[1]   Although mediation is in a formal sense the
weakest form of government intervention, it can frequently be
of great assistance, perhaps of more assistance than seemingly
stronger kinds of intervention.

Fact-finding lies somewhere between mediation and arbitration, differing from the latter in that it does not bind the parties
to accept the report of the fact-finders.   The name is perhaps
unfortunate, since it is seldom facts that are in dispute, but
rather the standards by which the relevance of various facts
are to be judged.   Whereas mediation works entirely behind
the scenes, the reports of fact-finders are usually made public,
and gain whatever strength they have by mobilizing public
opinion.

Fact-finding boards have been used frequently in recent years
in disputes creating a national emergency.   In some cases they
have been appointed by the President under his general
powers as chief executive.   In others they have been appointed
under the terms of the Taft-Hartley Act of 1947.   This act
provides for temporary (eighty-day) government seizure of
struck facilities in a strike that creates an emergency; during
this period the strikers return to work.   The fact-finding
board investigates the dispute but is not permitted to recom-
mend terms of settlement.

Fact-finding boards in the United States have frequently
failed to settle major disputes, and the strike has continued or
been resumed after the fact-finders have made their report.
Where the fact-finders have been successful in settling disputes
it is often because they have been functioning as high-level
mediators, commanding more respect from the parties than
the mediators ordinarily furnished by government agencies.
There is also much doubt about the value of the (eighty-day)
"cooling-off" period provided in the Taft-Hartley emergency
disputes procedure.   Where the main pressures for settlement
are the demands of customers on the employer and the need

[1] David L. Cole, "Government in the Bargaining Process: The Role
of Mediation," *Annals of the American Academy of Political and Social
Science*, January, 1961, p. 50.

of income to buy food and other necessities on the strikers, a "cooling-off" period can serve merely to delay the day when these pressures for settlement will be effective.

Many proposals have been made for having the government impose costs on the parties to emergency disputes so as to create an incentive to compromise. Seizure and operation under government control imposes costs on the workers if they are required to work under the terms of their old agreement, which they regard as unsatisfactory. If the government makes favorable changes in the terms of employment during seizure, this puts strong pressure on management to continue these terms. Higher costs could be imposed—for example, union dues or employer profits could be paid to the government during seizure. However, any such imposed costs will alter the outcome of the dispute by their uneven impact on the parties. No one has yet devised a scheme that would operate solely to hasten the very settlement that would have been reached without intervention.

Thus government intervention in strikes remains an area for improvisation and *ad hoc* solutions. Perhaps the chief power of government is that it can create uncertainty about its ultimate action. A party to the strike may then accept a known, if disagreeable, settlement in preference to an unknown outcome that has some chance of being much worse.

The key person in difficult strike situations is often the elected head of a government—a mayor, a governor, or the President of the United States. Few such officials would allow the votes or campaign contributions of unions or of management to determine the nature of their role. Yet even where they are not fully aware of it themselves, they may be influenced to some extent by the political power of the groups with which they deal. For this reason, the political power of unions is a source of strength somewhat apart from their economic ability to conduct a strike.[1]

[1] It may also be noted that the political influence of unions can be a source of strength in situations other than strikes. The building trades unions can often get their members appointed as building inspectors, and

§ 3. Wildcat Strikes and Slowdowns. A wildcat strike is one conducted in violation of an agreement or without proper authorization from higher union bodies—by a department or unit without authorization from the local union or by a local union without authorization from the national union. (In most unions such authorization is required.) Many wildcat strikes, especially spontaneous ones, arise from dissatisfaction with union policies and thus cannot be considered a source of union strength. At other times, however, a union may tacitly condone or encourage strikes that it officially disowns. Wildcat strikes sometimes occur during negotiations for a new agreement, when they may exert pressure for a quicker settlement.

It may seem odd that although spontaneous strikes of non-union workers are now rare, wildcat strikes by unionists are fairly common. One explanation is that the penalty for striking is less severe in the latter case. Unions will usually agree to employer discipline of workers who strike in violation of an agreement, but they will oppose penalties they regard as excessive. Some wildcat strikes occur when workers feel there is an immediate threat to their health or safety. If they cannot convince their supervisors of the danger, a wildcat strike is their only recourse. Union opposition to severe or automatic penalties for wildcat strikers is based in part on cases of this kind.

Some observers of industrial relations report a decreasing frequency of wildcat strikes in recent years. In part this may result from the maturing of union organizations and greater control of union members by their leaders. In part, it is reported to result from more severe and consistent use of discipline by management, since management often found

inspectors can be less exacting on union jobs than on non-union jobs. In licensed occupations such as plumbers, electricians, and barbers the unions sometimes nominate members of the licensing boards. If such boards deny licenses to qualified workers, they can help to raise the wages of license-holders. Setting qualifications higher than those needed to protect public health or safety will have similar effects.

that to settle a wildcat strike by making concessions invited the use of similar tactics in the future.[1]

We can regard the authorized strike as the heavy artillery of the trade union, and the wildcat strike and the slowdown as its small arms—weapons suited for limited engagements and local objectives. The slowdown is a temporary slackening of the normal pace of work designed to put pressure on management to gain some objective. The workers remain on the job and appear to be engaged in their usual activities.[2] "Slowdown" is a narrower term than restriction of output, which may be permanent. The ability to restrict output permanently is a consequence of having power to begin with, and not a source of additional power. For the slowdown to be effective as a pressure tactic, management must be aware of it. In contrast, restriction of output undertaken to prolong a job may be most successful if management is unaware of it.

The most frequent source of slowdowns is dissatisfaction with incentive wage rates, and grievances of this kind give rise to slowdowns in non-union as well as union plants. A slowdown is almost never formally authorized by a union but may be conducted with tacit union consent. Its advantage over the wildcat strike is the protection from discipline afforded the participants. In a well-run slowdown, management observes the reduction in output but cannot detect the subtle changes in work behavior that cause it and therefore cannot identify the individual participants.

§ 4. Consumer Boycotts and Union Labels. The consumer boycott and the union label are opposite sides of the same coin. A boycott urges consumers not to buy products made by non-union labor, whereas a union label on consumer goods encourages sympathetic shoppers to choose products made

[1] See Sumner H. Slichter, James J. Healy, and E. Robert Livernash, *The Impact of Collective Bargaining on Management* (Washington, D.C.: Brookings Institution, 1960), pp. 663–91.
[2] See R. S. Hammett, Joel Seidman, and Jack London, "The Slowdown as a Union Tactic," *Journal of Political Economy*, Vol. LXV (April, 1957).

under union conditions.   In general, these are weak weapons.
However, the consumer boycott is sometimes effective against
retail establishments in localities where union membership is
concentrated, and the union label has helped to organize
industries such as work clothing whose products are heavily
consumed by manual workers.   Where union strength rests
largely on the power to strike, the label can be of more value to
the customer than to the union.   Thus in most union print
shops, the label or "bug" is used only at the request of the
customer, yet little political campaign literature appears
without it.

The proper public attitude toward the union label would be
an important and difficult question if the weapon were more
powerful.   The principle that workers should be free to join
or not to join unions of their own choosing would seem to
require that they be free from consumer pressures as well as
from management pressures.   On the other hand, it can be
argued that consumer freedom extends to knowledge about the
working conditions under which products are made.   On this
view, the union label on a loaf of bread stands on the same
footing as the label that it contains artificial preservatives—
each may be of intense interest to some buyers and be totally
ignored by others.

§ 5. **Secondary Boycotts.**   The secondary boycott is a strike
or threat of strike in which the union's complaint is not against
the employer struck but against someone with whom he does
business.   For example, the workers in a retail store may
refuse to handle the products of a struck manufacturer.   If
their employer directs them to do so, they may walk out
altogether in an effort to force him to buy from another
supplier.

The use of the secondary boycott is now severely restricted
by law.   Some of the restrictions are part of the Landrum-
Griffin Act of 1959, which at this writing is still too recent to
permit any confident evaluation of their exact meaning or
effects.   The secondary boycott is one of a group of related

devices that include organizational picketing, sympathetic strikes, "hot cargo" clauses, and the respecting of picket lines set up by other unions. All these devices may now be illegal in interstate commerce under most circumstances. The meaning of some of the terms used above can be conveyed by the examples that follow.

Perhaps the simplest form of secondary boycott is the refusal to do struck work; thus if the molders' union strikes a job foundry, union molders at other foundries would refuse to fill orders for the struck employer. This example differs from the retail store example given above because the relation between the two employers is horizontal rather than vertical.

Secondary boycotts and hot cargo clauses can also be used for organizational purposes. If the employees of a certain trucker cannot be organized, hot cargo clauses in union agreements with other truckers are used to prevent them from handling transfer shipments to or from the non-union firm. Since such action could often force the non-union firm out of business, its employees are forced to change their minds and join the union to preserve their jobs. This union action interferes with the right of workers to organize or not to organize as they see fit if the individual employer is considered to be the proper unit for employee selection of a bargaining agent.

In perhaps the most objectionable case, a union will refuse to handle products made by members of another union. Thus the sheet metal workers' union has refused to install products made by members of the steelworkers' union. Here the object is not to force the steelworkers to change unions, but to get more work for another group of workers already organized by the sheet metal workers.

It is sometimes hard to distinguish between a secondary boycott and a consumer boycott. If pickets appear before a non-union service station with signs urging customers not to buy, these signs may have little effect on the customers. However, union teamsters may refuse to deliver gas and thus can force the station to close. The definition of a secondary boycott should not depend on externals like the wording of the picket sign, but on the consequences of the picketing. Although there is a tradition in the labor movement against crossing picket lines, most union members follow the instructions of their leaders in such matters. If teamsters all refuse to cross a certain picket line, there has probably been an arrangement between their local and the striking union. It then seems reasonable to conclude that the teamsters' local as an organization is engaged in a secondary boycott.[1]

A horizontal secondary boycott is one in which the primary and secondary employer are engaged in the same type of activity, as in the "hot cargo" and foundry examples above. The purpose of such boycotts is reasonably clear. Low wages in one plant in an industry may give it a competitive advantage. The union will seek to raise these wages if the plant is organized and to organize it if it is not. This action will be of direct benefit to union members elsewhere in helping to preserve their jobs and their wage levels, and their participation in the boycott can be explained by self-interest.

Where the relation between the primary and secondary employer is vertical—if, for example, the latter buys supplies from the former—the purpose of the secondary boycott is more complex. In some cases, the boycott may be entirely sympathetic, arising out of a feeling of solidarity among workers. If the union seeks to raise the costs of the primary employer, the boycotting workers of the secondary employer are acting against their economic self-interest. Higher costs of materials to their employer will tend to reduce his sales and his ability to offer employment or wage increases. The action of the boycotting unionists might then be affected by one or more of the following considerations: (1) They may not understand the way in which higher costs of materials are detrimental to them. (2) They or their leaders may consider that having a large union or a large labor movement is worth

[1] Following the passage of the Landrum-Griffin Act in 1959, the teamsters' union instructed its locals not to respect the picket lines of other unions.

the possible costs of shorter hours or smaller wage increases. (3) They may benefit from some financial device within the union by which employees of the supplier pay more than their fair share of a pension or welfare fund that benefits employees of the purchaser. For example, workers who instal sheet-metal work might benefit from a welfare fund to which manufacturing workers in the same union contribute heavily. This last consideration is appealing if we seek to explain behavior entirely in economic terms, but I know of no evidence supporting it.

§ 6. **Control of the Labor Supply.** The control of the labor supply is often considered to be a source of union power. The term can have several meanings. Most of those that apply to true unions, as distinguished from union-like organizations, have already been covered under other headings.

The most effective type of control of the labor supply is control over the number of people who can be trained for an occupation or profession. By limiting the number trained, the organization can protect or raise the earnings of its members. There is strong evidence that the American Medical Association has had such power,[1] but it is doubtful whether any organization ordinarily considered a union possesses similar power. Craft unions often operate apprenticeship programs in co-operation with employers and require employers under most circumstances to give preference in employment to those who complete such programs. However, union apprenticeship programs do not by any means train all of the journeymen in the skilled trades. Many workers pick up their skill on the job in non-union employment, especially in smaller communities. They may later move into union employment, for few unions will deny membership to all those not trained in union apprenticeship programs. While such a source of supply exists, the union

[1] See Milton Friedman and Simon Kuznets, *Income from Independent Professional Practice* (New York: National Bureau of Economic Research, 1945), pp. 8–21 and 118–37.

cannot effectively limit entry to the trade by limiting the number of apprentices of union employers or unduly lengthening the period of apprenticeship.

The closed shop, which requires employers to hire only union members, is sometimes considered to be a control of the labor supply, but this view seems forced where qualified non-union members are available. It would be better to say that the union, by its power to strike, denies the employer access to part of the supply so that he is forced to choose between operating solely with union labor and solely with non-union labor. Of course, the union's power to strike is increased if there are few non-union workers in a trade and if these are reluctant to work for struck employers. The closed shop will be considered further in Chapter VI.

The case of union representation on licensing boards is more nearly like the case of medicine. Licensing has been mentioned earlier (see footnote on pp. 40–41) as an exercise of union political power.

CHAPTER III

UNION WAGE POLICY

§ 1. The Meaning of Wage Policy.   The union's power to win concessions from employers can be used to increase wages and to reach non-monetary goals.   This chapter and the two that follow will deal with wages;   later chapters will deal with non-wage aspects of bargaining.

The term wage policy refers here to the formulation of goals for which the union is prepared to fight.   It does not refer to the announcement of initial bargaining demands, which are usually well in excess of what the union expects to get.   These are designed largely to gain tactical advantages in bargaining, to influence public opinion, or to demonstrate to the members that their officers are trying to carry out the members' instructions.   The outcome of wage negotiations, of course, does not depend solely on union wage policy.   Employer policy must also be considered, and often government policy as well.   Behind these proximate factors lie many complex economic and political forces.

Within the union, the determination of wage policy is largely a leadership function, though the leaders are sensitive to the temper of the members, and often have the difficult job of formulating acceptable compromises among the demands of diverse groups within the membership.   The members or committees representing them sometimes assist in formulating initial demands, but the union negotiators must decide whether and when to retreat from these.   In some unions,

48

wage agreements must be ratified by the members, but rejection of an agreement approved by the union negotiators is rather rare.

As mentioned in Chapter I, wage policy is formed at different levels in different unions. In industries with national product markets like coal and steel, it is formed by the national union; in local market industries it is usually formed by local unions. Mixed and intermediate cases can also be found.

§ 2. Wage Goals.

The classic statement of union wage objectives is that unions always want more. Under very adverse circumstances when employers seek wage cuts, the union can be reduced to holding the line, but even this can be considered as wanting more—more than the employer wants to pay and more than non-union workers are getting.

For the economist, this statement of the union's goal is not very satisfying. How much more? The theory of the business firm suggests precise answers to the analogous question about the prices of products. The firm raises prices until net profit (the difference between total receipts and total costs) is at a maximum and then it stops. If the initial price should happen to be above the price that would maximize profits, the firm will reduce prices, not raise them. Some economists have argued that the union, too, must be attempting to maximize something.[1] We shall see, however, that attempts to define what the union maximizes have so far been rather unsatisfactory.

Even for the firm, the concept of maximizing runs into some difficulties. Industries with monopoly power sometimes set prices below those at which they could sell their full-capacity output, as the steel and automobile industries did for several years after World War II. In such cases firms are not maximizing net profits in the short run. They can be viewed as

---

[1] "An economic theory of a trade union requires that the organization be assumed to maximize (or minimize) something." John T. Dunlop, *Wage Determination under Trade Unions* (New York: Macmillan Co., 1944), p. 4.

maximizing some long-run net profit by conserving the customer's good will, or avoiding government regulation, but here the concept of maximizing grows imprecise. At the limit, the hypothesis that the firm is maximizing long-run profit becomes a tautology. Sometimes the only evidence that the policy pursued will maximize profits in the long run is that the firm has chosen to pursue it, and this assumes the conclusion. To avoid such circularity, maximizing behavior must have observable consequences so that, at least in principle, departures from maximizing behavior can be detected and the hypothesis is not logically irrefutable.

Despite these reservations, the concept of profit-maximization has proved its worth for the competitive firm, and provides at least a useful point of departure for the monopoly. The controversy has narrowed to two basic positions—that monopolistic firms maximize net profit and that they do not. In the union case, we have, on the one hand, the view that unions do not maximize anything, and, on the other, several different proposed maximands.

§ 3. The Demand for Union Labor.

To discuss maximizing models of union wage policy, we must assume the existence of a downward-sloping demand curve for union labor. This curve can be shown on a graph representing the demand for labor in an industry or craft on which the hourly wage rate is plotted against the vertical axis and the number of union members employed is plotted against the horizontal axis (see Fig., p. 51). Wages in other industries or crafts are assumed to remain unchanged. The demand curve runs from the upper left-hand corner of the graph down toward the lower right. It is to be interpreted as showing the number of union members employers will choose to employ at each wage with unchanged demand for their product. (For convenience, it is assumed that at all wages, each man works the same number of hours per week.) If the number of men employed were not dependent on the wage rate, the curve would be a vertical line. However, as the union raises wages, it will in fact set in motion

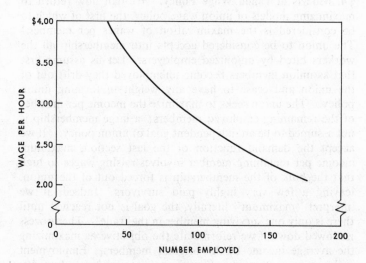

A Hypothetical Demand Curve for Union Labor

forces tending to reduce the number of members at work. If the industry is not completely organized, non-union firms will expand at the expense of union firms. In any case, the employers using the least labor to produce a given output will tend to expand at the expense of others. Moreover, each employer will have an incentive to use more or better equipment or more supervision or perhaps better materials to cut down his use of the labor whose price has risen. Finally, as the price of the product rises, the consumer will tend to use less of it and will turn instead to substitute products.

The forces listed above can be weak or strong. Where they are strong, a small percentage increase in the wage will cause a large percentage fall in employment and the demand is then said to be elastic. If the forces reducing employment are weak, a small percentage increase in the wage will cause a smaller percentage decrease in employment. The demand is then said to be inelastic.

§ 4. Models of Union Wage Policy.

We can now return to maximizing models of union wage policy, the first of which to be considered is the maximization of wages per member.[1] The union to be considered accepts into membership all the workers hired by unionized employers. Let us assume first that as union members become unemployed they drift out of the union and cease to have any weight in forming union policy. The union seeks to maximize the income per member of the remaining employed members; a large membership is not assumed to be an independent goal of union policy. If we accept the demand function of the last section, maximum income per remaining member involves raising wages so high that the bulk of the membership is forced out of the union, leaving a few very highly paid survivors. Indeed, if we interpret "maximum" literally, the goal is not reached until there is only one surviving member in the trade! The process is slowed down if we reformulate the objective as maximizing the average income of the original members. Employment will now be contracted only at the rate at which members die, retire, or resign, but the eventual outcome will be the same.

There is only one important actual case that lends support to this model—that of the United Mine Workers. Even in this case the loss of employment cannot be wholly ascribed to the union's wage policy, although the Mine Workers have pursued a high-wage policy in the face of shrinking employment with announced unconcern. In general, however, loss of employment and membership does act as a check on wage demands. This is reasonable even if the union's objective is viewed simply as some average of the objectives of the members considered individually. The employed members have ties of friendship and sympathy with those who become unemployed. They may want their sons or nephews to succeed them in the

---

[1] This model has been put forward in Henry C. Simons, "Some Reflections on Syndicalism" in *Economic Policy for a Free Society* (Chicago: University of Chicago Press, 1948), especially pp. 131–32, and in Charles E. Lindblom, *Unions and Capitalism* (New Haven, Conn.: Yale University Press, 1949), especially Chapter VI.

trade. It is not the height of rationality to say "*après moi le déluge.*"

If we consider the union as an institution with leaders and goals of its own, the model just presented becomes still less tenable. It is almost a universal characteristic of organizations that they seek to survive even when they have fulfilled their original purposes. A leader seeks to expand his organization because this increases his prestige, power, and self-esteem, and not infrequently his salary as well. The members may also derive satisfaction from belonging to a large and growing organization.

When the extent of union organization was low, losses of members in one area could be regained by organizing another area. As unions have grown, this has become increasingly difficult. A policy of very high wages may thus lose more membership from the area already organized than it can gain through helping to extend the union's jurisdiction. The policy will then conflict with the organizational goals of the union and the personal goals of its leaders.

If we recognize both high wages and large membership as union goals, it is tempting to combine them in a single quantity to be maximized. This is done in models that suggest that the union seeks to maximize the wage bill—the aggregate wages received by the entire membership.[1] But this goal is obviously unrealistic where the demand for union labor is elastic and the union has already raised wages. In such situations, a wage reduction would increase the wage bill because the percentage increase in membership would be larger than the percentage reduction in wages per member, and this would continue to be true until the wage was back to the non-union level. Although the demand for union labor will in fact be elastic where there is strong competition from non-union labor, we do not observe unions in such situations asking for wage cuts. The goal of maximizing wages per member is deficient because it implies that unions have no concern for members who become unemployed and no interest in remaining in

[1] See Dunlop, *op. cit.*, Chapter III.

existence as organizations. The goal of maximizing the wage
bill has the opposite difficulty—it implies that unions can be
interested in increasing membership to the point of leaving
the original members no better off than they would have been
without a union.

Perhaps the most realistic assumption we can make is that
unions are interested both in raising wages and in having a
large membership, but that the precise weights to be attached
to these two objectives will differ from union to union and
from time to time. A special significance must be attached
to the initial position in formulating future strategy. The
union will generally be more willing to fight to prevent cuts in
present wages than to win increases, and it will be more
concerned about preserving the employment of present members than about enlarging the membership. This formulation
falls short of achieving a single maximand corresponding to
profits for the firm. At the same time, it suggests that many
union wage policies can be viewed within a reasonably simple
framework of rational behavior.

In pursuing their goals, unions must also take account of the
costs of alternative wage policies. More work needs to be done
in specifying the kinds of costs that need to be considered here,
though the costs of strikes are one obvious factor, as are the
costs of encouraging the growth of non-union competition.

§ 5. **Pressures on Wage Decisions.** The discussion of §§ 2 and
4 is intended to explain to those familiar with other branches
of economics why we cannot use precisely the kind of tools to
which they are accustomed. This does not mean that
economists can say nothing about union wage policy, but only
that they must work within a somewhat loose framework.

The rest of this chapter will consider union wage policy as
formed by two sets of forces. The first is the pressure for
higher wages generated by the wants and aspirations of the
members and the ambitions of their leaders. This desire for
higher wages can be mobilized by political, occupational, or
geographical groups within the union so that it reaches the top

leadership in the form of political pressures. The desire of union members and of groups within the union for higher wages is not felt or expressed continuously; a wage increase will often satisfy it for a while. However, as the level of income rises elsewhere and as members get accustomed to their new standard of living, their reach once more comes to exceed their grasp, and pressures for "more" reassert themselves. Union leaders often anticipate this process, so that the members may not be aware of any dissatisfaction until the leaders formulate new goals and defend them as just or reasonable expectations. Both for members and leaders, these expectations are usually formed by comparison with other wage rates—they take the form of believing that "we" are entitled to as much as "they" have gotten.

The pressures for higher wages are contained by economic constraints in the union's environment and by employer resistance. Sometimes these constraints will have the effect of convincing the union that it could not win a strike or could win only a Pyrrhic victory. At other times the union will become convinced that a wage increase would cause undesirable reductions in hours or employment. If employment or hours are already falling, the preservation of employment will become the union's chief concern, and it may not attempt to change existing wages for long periods.

The interaction of these political and economic forces is quite different when employment is rising and when it is falling. The two cases will be considered separately.

§ 6. Wage Policy When Employment Is Rising. Periods of rising employment, especially if accompanied by rising prices, offer unions the greatest freedom from economic constraints. Even in such periods, however, wage increases will usually have an effect on employment. But the effect will take the form not of an absolute reduction in employment, but of a reduction in its rate of growth, and such an effect is less likely than an absolute reduction to be perceived by the union. (It is, indeed, often overlooked by economists.) If it is perceived, it will, nevertheless, not usually be an effective check on wage demands. As I have argued above, the union is concerned about preserving employment for present members and it usually wants to grow. But it is not likely to make large sacrifices to maintain a rapid rate of growth—to win benefits for people whom it cannot yet identify.[1]

In periods of rising employment and prices, employers will be more willing to grant wage increases for at least two reasons. First, their losses from strikes will usually be greater at such times. Second, a wage increase can be useful to employers in tight labor markets in recruiting and holding adequate numbers of qualified workers. Nevertheless, employers often resist wage demands even when the labor market is tight. They may fear that the tight labor market will only be temporary, and that they will be unable to reduce the high union wage scale when it is no longer useful. They may also fear that they are contributing to inflation, or are thought to do so by the public, when they raise wages. Large corporations may be quite sensitive to criticism on this score from the press, the government, or other parts of the business community. We will return to the question of wages and inflation in Chapter V. In periods when economic constraints and employer resistance are weak the political forces working towards uniform wage increases have freest play. Thus from 1945 to 1948, the high level of demand for products and labor, and the high level of profits of most employers eliminated union fears of reductions in employment, and permitted employers to pass on wage increases in the form of higher prices. A rising cost of living, affecting all unions similarly, heightened the pressure for wage increases. Under these conditions, the first major wage agreement in any period of contract renewal tended to set a pattern that was widely followed in other bargains. The result was three "rounds" of wage increases that were virtually uniform in timing and

[1] This view would have to be modified if the union starts from a position where some of the members are unemployed and are guaranteed preference in hiring.

amount for large firms in several industries, including basic steel, automobiles, agricultural implements, electrical machinery, rubber, and metal mining.

There was undoubtedly an important political factor in this uniformity of wage increases. In a period of intense rivalry between unions and bitter factionalism within them, a leader who settled with a prosperous firm for less than the pattern would have provided potent ammunition to his opponents. As one observer has put it, the political pressures created "orbits of coercive comparison."[1]

Although the concept of coercive comparisons is an apt one in the context that gave rise to it, it should not be pushed too far. Where comparisons collide with strong economic constraints, the constraints are still more coercive. Even in periods of prosperity and rising prices, two reservations must be noted. First, wage settlements usually include some changes in wage supplements or "fringe benefits" whose exact value is difficult to determine. The announced cost of these fringes is sometimes manipulated to create a misleading impression of uniformity in the total "package" from one settlement to another. Second, it is only the exact uniformity of the wage settlements that needs to be explained in political terms. Their general similarity can be explained by broad economic forces, such as the rising cost of living, and the strong demand for labor in all industries. In such circumstances, money wage increases in non-union industries may be quite similar to and may often precede the principal union wage settlements.

In some periods of rising employment we can observe union wages that seem to be below the rates that would prevail in a non-union market in the short run. There are two kinds of evidence of such a condition—the payment of rates above the union scale and labor shortages that cause union employers to go to considerable expense and trouble to recruit workers. Conditions of this sort have been common in Scandinavia,

[1] Arthur M. Ross, *Trade Union Wage Policy* (Berkeley and Los Angeles: University of California Press, 1948), Chapter III.

where they have given rise to the term "wage drift"—the excess of the rise in average earnings over the rise in union rates. There is little evidence of wage drift in the United States, with the principal exception of the building trades, where workers are not uncommonly paid more than the union scale. Some part of this excess is payment for exceptional ability. Labor shortages in unionized industries are less uncommon; in 1946–47 they seem to have been rather wide-spread.

The existence of "wage drift" and labor shortages in unionized employment may result from the imperfect foresight of the union. For example, an agreement setting wages for a fixed period may have been concluded just before the demand for labor increased. At other times unions may choose not to exert their full power. But if the employer is concerned about the future results of a wage agreement, even the strong use of union power may not persuade him to agree to long-term rates high enough to eliminate labor shortages that he believes are temporary.

§ 7. Wage Policy When Employment Is Falling. When employment is falling, economic constraints press closely on the union and there is little room for political maneuvering in the formation of wage policy. In times of adversity, rival factions in a union or rival unions in an industry may in effect agree to forego wage increases and not to use the lack of gains as a political issue.

Employment of union members can fall for a variety of reasons. Perhaps the most frequent is a contraction in general business activity, which ordinarily causes sharp drops in employment in mining, railroads, and the manufacture of durable goods. Early in the history of American unionism, a frequent employer response to a depression was to refuse to deal with unions and to seek to return to non-union conditions. As we have seen, many unions went out of existence at such times; others lost control of much of their jurisdiction. As unions became stronger and better accepted, the employer more often continued to recognize the union during a depression, but sought to negotiate wage cuts.　Sometimes the union accepted these cuts, often after drawing out negotiations to preserve the old rate for as long as possible.　There were sometimes strikes to avert a wage cut or reduce its amount, though strikes of this sort were fought under conditions that seldom favored the union.

Since World War II the relative mildness of recessions, the upward drift of prices, and the growing acceptance of unions have created a climate in which cyclical contractions have caused almost no cuts in wage rates.　Instead, they produce either agreements to retain the old rates or wage increases of smaller than average size.　Unions reluctant to strike during a recession have attempted to extend agreements until a more favorable time for seeking gains.　In the summer of 1958, members of the United Automobile Workers worked for several months after the expiration of an agreement without any extension.　A new agreement was negotiated only after the beginning of a model year and an improvement of business conditions had increased the union's bargaining power.

Wage cuts are still possible in exceptional circumstances, especially if the union views a worsening of conditions as permanent.　Such permanent changes can include the introduction of processes and equipment that displace union members, the expansion of the non-union sector of a partially organized industry, or the decline of a whole industry because of changes in consumer tastes.　Even under highly adverse conditions, it is hard for a union to accept the necessity for a wage cut.　It takes an exceptionally close and trusting relationship between management and the union over a period of years to permit union leaders to convince the members that a wage cut is necessary.[1]　Some wage cuts have resulted from the binding arbitration of wage disputes, particularly in the New England cotton textile industry, which has been under

[1] For an interesting study of this point, see Irwin L. Herrnstadt, "The Reaction of Three Local Unions to Economic Adversity," *Journal of Political Economy*, October, 1954.

strong pressure from non-union competition from the South. Arbitrated wage cuts permit the union leadership to blame the wage cut on the arbitrator, even though the leaders might privately concede the wisdom of his decision.

The downward inflexibility of union wage rates in recessions does not mean that wage costs per unit are also inflexible downward. Tighter administration of piece-rate systems and incentive wage systems under such conditions often produces lower unit costs without any formal change in the rates. Under time rates, the same effect could be produced by greater employee effort. The impact of a recession on worker effort will depend on the balance between forces leading the workers to try to stretch out the work to make it last and forces leading them to try to reduce costs in order to get more business for the firm. The latter might be expected to predominate in competitive industries.

§ 8. **Wage Policy toward Individual Firms.** The preceding discussion has been largely concerned with union wage policy for industries or jurisdictions as a whole. Unions are faced with somewhat different problems when a particular employer is in economic difficulties.

Unions in highly competitive industries, especially those for which wages are a large part of the cost of production, will almost always pursue a standard wage policy within a given product market. They set uniform time rates or piece rates for all firms so as "to take labor out of competition." The building trades and printing trades set standard time rates within each local product market. Unions in the clothing industry have attempted to equalize unit labor costs over wider areas. In such industries, unions cannot make special wage concessions to one employer without threatening their whole wage structure, for other employers would insist on similar concessions. Instead, the union may seek to help improve the efficiency of a firm in economic difficulties.

The situation is quite different for unions that bargain with diverse employers selling in different product markets. Thus the United Steelworkers pursues a standard wage policy in bargaining with the big companies in the basic steel industry but is much more flexible in dealing with the many kinds of steel fabricators with whom it bargains. Similarly, the United Auto Workers tries to preserve uniformity of wage increases among the three major automobile producers, but permits diversity of wages in the firms making parts and components.[1] In both cases, the diversity in wage levels and wage changes is greatest for the firms that lie furthest, geographically or industrially, from the heart of the union's jurisdiction, and is greater during recessions than in more prosperous years.

Unions with this kind of wage policy can permit deviations from their wage pattern if these do not create a competitive threat to employment in other firms organized by the union, and this is likely to be true if products are highly specialized. Local unions may favor such concessions to firms in financial trouble, either because the members fear reductions in hours and employment, or because loss of income from previous layoffs has made them reluctant to strike.

Although there is ample evidence that such unions as the auto workers and the steelworkers permit wage diversity within their jurisdictions, a more difficult question remains unanswered. We do not know whether this diversity is similar to that which would exist in a non-union situation, or whether despite remaining differentials, the union has compressed the structure of wage rates among firms.

§ 9. Wage Structure. The wage differentials among firms just discussed are one aspect of wage structure about which unions may have a policy. Several other aspects are also important, including geographical and occupational differentials.

Much of union policy in the area of geographical, sex, and

[1] See George Seltzer, "Pattern Bargaining and the United Steelworkers," *Journal of Political Economy*, August, 1951; George Seltzer, "The United Steelworkers and Unionwide Bargaining," *Monthly Labor Review*, February 1961; and Harold M. Levinson, "Pattern Bargaining: A Case Study of the Automobile Workers, "*Quarterly Journal of Economics*, May, 1960.

race differentials can be summed up in the slogan "equal pay for equal work," which has an important place in union ideology.   It will be discussed here in reference to geographical differentials.   The elimination of these differentials is supported by two forces in addition to equalitarian social philosophy—political pressures from the low-paid groups, and the fear of loss of employment by the high-paid groups. Unions in national product markets often eliminate geographical differentials through centralized bargaining at the firm level (with multiplant firms) or at the industry level.   In industries with local product markets, local unions in low-wage areas pursue the goal of equality as best they can.   Here the pressure toward equality from the high-paid areas is absent, since these areas are not threatened by the competition of low-wage areas. The remaining pressures toward wage equalization are generally rather weak.

The concept of equal pay for equal work also has a central place in the economic theory of the labor market but a somewhat different one than in union tradition.   Economic theory views equality of compensation (wages and other net benefits of employment) as a result of the most efficient allocation of labor—the allocation in which no worker could increase his productivity by moving.   If one area has a relatively plentiful supply of labor it will tend to have low wages for workers of given efficiency and these low wages will be an inducement for workers to leave the area and for employers to enter (under conditions of reasonably full employment in the high-wage areas).   Such movements of capital and labor on a large enough scale would eliminate the wage differentials and increase the total output of the economy.   If a union eliminates the wage differential by use of bargaining power while these resource movements are still going on, it eliminates the incentive for further movement.   Indeed this is a major part of the appeal of the policy of equality to the union member in the high-wage area.   He especially does not want employers in his area to transfer operations to areas where wages are lower.

Unions may sometimes equalize wage rates where the

original differentials were based on the lower efficiency of the low-paid workers. In these cases, the equal wages create an incentive for the shift of employment toward the former high-paid areas. On the whole, however, the available evidence suggests that this kind of effect of union policy is probably not very important. Geographical wage differentials in the United States are based largely on differences in the abundance of labor supply rather than on differences in the efficiency of manual workers.[1] A more abundant labor supply leads to low wages and leads employers to use more labor relative to capital. The contribution of labor to production at the margin will then be lower than in the high-wage areas even with no differences in worker capacities.

The difference between the traditions of economic theorists and trade unionists on geographical wage differentials can be summarized in this way: The economist puts primary emphasis on efficiency, and views "equal pay for equal work" as a pleasant by-product of achieving efficient allocation. The unionist, for a combination of idealistic and selfish reasons, puts primary emphasis on geographical equality. He is either unaware of the loss of efficiency from achieving equality too soon (as the economist views it), or considers this a reasonable price to pay for achieving his primary goal.

Union policy on occupational wage differentials is different in craft and in industrial unions. In industries where each craft union represents a different occupation, there can be no policy on occupational differentials as such. They will be whatever results from the operation of the economic environment and the bargaining power and strategies of the various

---

[1] See D. Gale Johnson, "Comparability of Labor Capacities of Farm and Nonfarm Labor," *American Economic Review*, Vol. XLII (June, 1953), and Robert E. Weintraub, "The Productive Capacity of Rural and Urban Labor: A Case Study," *Journal of Political Economy*, Vol. LXIII (October, 1955). For an account of a case in which union compression of wage differentials failed to offset the attraction of higher productivity in the low-wage areas, see Irvin Sobel "Collective Bargaining and Decentralization in the Rubber Tire Industry," *Journal of Political Economy*, Vol. LXII (February, 1954).

unions.   In face of a strong long-run trend toward the narrowing of relative differentials among occupations in the economy
as a whole, some unions of highly paid craftsmen seem to have
been successful in limiting the narrowing of differentials in
their industry.   Where several crafts are represented in one
craft union, the highest paid crafts often dominate the internal
politics of the union, which again suggests the likelihood of a
policy of resisting the narrowing of differentials.

In industrial unions, on the other hand, the highly paid
crafts are usually in a minority.   Such unions often adopt a
policy of reducing relative differentials among occupations,
principally by bargaining for "across-the-board" wage
increases of a stated number of cents per hour at all wage levels.
However, when the levelling policies of industrial unions out-
run the underlying economic forces making for greater equality,
important counterpressures are soon felt.   The United
Automobile Workers has had to negotiate special wage
increases for skilled workers on more than one occasion.
Some of its skilled members have at times threatened to petition
the National Labor Relations Board to create separate bargaining units for them as a way of putting pressure on their union.
In a dramatic case of protest against wage levelling, the motor-
men in the New York City subway system temporarily broke
away from their industrial union, formed a separate craft
union, and conducted an effective strike for the widening of
occupational differentials.

In the area of occupational differentials, industrial unions
face strong political pressures based on concepts of equity.
But these concepts of equity are not static—they are themselves
slowly but surely influenced by the economic climate.   Thus
they respond to such forces as changes in the level of education
of the labor force, which is one of the major underlying
determinants of occupational wage structure.   The unionization of an industry does not lead to the replacement of
economic by political forces in the setting of wages; rather,
the economic forces are filtered through political groupings,
which can delay or redirect them but not reverse their flow.

§ 10. Methods of Wage Payment. Three principal methods
of wage payment are common in various parts of American
industry: time rates, piece rates, and incentive rates. Under
time rates, the worker is paid by the hour and the employer
attempts to insure a reasonable output through the mechanical
pacing of operations or through supervision and discipline for
inadequate performance. Under piece rates, which are
common in the shoe and apparel industries, workers are paid
a specified rate or price for each unit of output they produce.
In an incentive rate system, pay is based in part on the rate
of output, but is not exactly proportional to it. Ordinarily,
there is a guaranteed base rate below which hourly earnings
cannot fall. Incentive plans can cover groups of workers or
whole establishments rather than individuals.

The attitude of unions toward these various methods of
wage payment varies widely. Some unions, such as the
United Automobile Workers, have traditionally favored time
rates and opposed incentive plans. Others, such as the
United Steelworkers have permitted or even encouraged
the growth of incentive plans in their industries. Unions in the
traditional piece-rate industries have long bargained in terms
of piece rates for particular jobs and tasks. However, a few
attitudes are common to all systems. Unions do not regard
the determination of performance standards or piece or incentive rates as a unilateral management function; they reserve
the right to protest the establishment of rates they regard as
unfair. Ordinarily, they will not allow the changing of an
established or agreed rate or standard except when there is a
change in the nature of the work. Moreover, they take a
skeptical attitude toward the use of time-study and other
industrial engineering techniques in the establishment of
standards and rates. While they almost always permit the
use of these techniques, they do not regard the results as
a strictly scientific basis for wage determination, but rather
as an art whose outcome will vary with the practitioner.
Some unions have their own time-study and industrial
engineering staffs, which can be used to challenge the findings

of management engineers or even to help set rates where management has no engineering staff of its own.

When union policies make it very hard for management to make changes in incentive wage systems, the systems sometimes get "demoralized" and produce very high earnings for modest effort. Under such circumstances, it becomes a difficult task for management to negotiate the revision of the incentive system or its replacement by time rates, and sometimes this can only be accomplished when there is a danger of the failure of the firm or the relocation of the plant.[1]

§ 11. Fringe Benefits.   Wage supplements or "fringe benefits" have become an important part of the total compensation of wage-earners.   These fringe benefits include those provided by law, those unilaterally introduced by employers, and those obtained by unions through collective bargaining.   Where employees are represented by a union, the employer's obligation to bargain has been interpreted by the courts to extend to fringe benefits as well as wages.

The private fringe benefits, as distinguished from those provided by law, include employer contributions to pension funds, life insurance, disability insurance, and medical care plans.   If wages or earnings are defined (as they usually are) per hour paid for and not per hour worked, then fringe benefits will include payments for time not worked: holidays, vacations, sick leave, call-in pay, and several minor forms of paid leave.   All of these forms of private fringe benefits for wage-earners have grown rapidly in the past twenty years, a period in which unions have also grown rapidly.   There is some statistical evidence suggesting that the growth of fringe benefits has been particularly rapid in unionized employment.

One might expect union leaders to want to take an increasing

[1] For a very thorough discussion of the operation of various wage-payment systems under collective bargaining, see Sumner H. Slichter, James J. Healy, and E. Robert Livernash, *The Impact of Collective Bargaining on Management* (Washington, D.C.: Brookings Institution, 1960), Chapters XVII and XVIII.

portion of their bargaining gain in the form of fringe benefits, since they can get credit for innovation in this area. For example, the first union to win a third week of vacation after twenty years' service made a dramatic gain for its long-service members and for the organization. If the cost of these longer vacations had been distributed as a wage increase to all wage-earners, it would have seemed a piddling gain and not a novel one. Certainly unions have innovated in such areas as pensions for wage-earners and supplementary unemployment benefits, and these innovations have probably helped to increase benefit levels under public social insurance systems.

It must be recognized, however, that these have also been strong independent forces inducing employers to give wage increases in the form of fringe benefits. Enjoyment of many such benefits is related to length of service, and this relation is valuable to the employer in reducing the costs of voluntary labor turnover. From the point of view of the economy at large there may not be a corresponding reduction of costs, since fringe benefits, especially pension plans, can impede the flow of labor toward the uses where its productivity is highest. Both the benefit to the employer and the possible cost to the economy[1] are removed if the rights to an employer's contribution to pensions are vested in the employee, so that he can take it with him when he moves. This right is common for college professors and is rapidly becoming common for long-service workers under negotiated wage agreements.

The second important force working to increase the level of fringe benefits is the high level of the personal income tax in recent years. Gains taken as increased leisure rather than increased money income are not taxed, while employer contributions to pensions and insurance either are not taxed or are taxed on a preferential basis. By increasing fringe benefits rather than wages the employer can give his employees more

---

[1] There will not be a cost to the economy from fringe-benefit arrangements that reduce mobility if these arrangements are necessary to induce employers to invest in training their workers, thus raising the workers' productivity.

income after taxes at the same cost to himself. The trend toward higher fringe benefits thus seems to result from union policy, government policy, and worker preferences all working powerfully in the same direction.

CHAPTER IV

THE INFLUENCE OF UNIONS ON
RELATIVE EARNINGS

§1. **Predictions from Economic Theory.** The discussion of
union wage policy in the last chapter dealt with what unions
try to do about wages under various circumstances, considered primarily from the point of view of the union as an
organization. We now look at the union effect on relative
wages from the outside, seeking to find out how well unions
achieve their wage objectives and what consequences their
impact on wages has.

In judging the consequences of union wage effects, we shall
seek to compare the operation of organized labor markets with
the operation of unorganized labor markets as they exist in the
United States, for it would be unfair to compare the organized
market with some theoretical model of a perfect market that
has never existed. This effort will involve making implicit
judgments about the extent and nature of imperfections, such
as lack of knowledge, and barriers to mobility in unorganized
markets. In my opinion, such imperfections are pervasive
and are important in the short run, but in the long run market
forces operate rather effectively.

The term relative wages, which was introduced above, refers
to comparisons between wages under union and non-union
conditions. Thus a relative wage gain of 10 per cent will mean
that union members receive a wage 10 per cent higher than that
of comparable non-union workers. At this point little will be

said about whether relative gains are made wholly by raising
the level of union wages with non-union wages unchanged
(which would imply a rise in the general level of wages), or
whether they are made in part by a reduction in the wage that
non-union workers would get in the absence of unions any-
where.   The discussion of the general level of wages is reserved
for the following chapter.

This section is addressed to two general kinds of question.
First, why is it that the general order of effects of a successful
union seems to be in the neighborhood of 10 or 20 per cent
rather than, say, 1 or 2 per cent or even 100 or 200 per cent?
What kinds of forces limit the success of unions that temporarily achieve very large gains and drive them back toward
a more usual impact on relative wages?   The second question
is: what forces determine which unions will be successful and
which will be relatively unsuccessful?

The predictions of economic theory about the union impact
on relative wages are based on the elasticity of demand for
union labor, a concept that was introduced in Chapter III,
§ 2.   In particular, these predictions follow from the theory of
derived demand developed by Alfred Marshall.[1]   The term
"derived demand" is used to indicate that the demand for
labor is derived from the demand for the final product and the
supply of the other factors of production.   The more inelastic
the demand for union labor, the smaller the effect of a given
wage increase on employment and therefore the larger the
probable influence of a union on relative wages.

Marshall listed four conditions that affect the demand for
union labor.   The demand is more inelastic (1) the more
essential is union labor to the production of the final product,
(2) the more inelastic the demand for the final product, (3) the
smaller the ratio of the cost of union labor to the total cost of
the product, and (4) the more inelastic the supply of the other
factors of production.

Condition 1 means that there should be no good substitutes

[1] *Principles of Economics* (8th ed.; New York: Macmillan Co., 1920),
pp. 383–86.

for union labor in the production process.   In the short run,
this means that employers should not be able to replace union
members with new non-union workers or with supervisory
personnel.   In the long run, the possibilities for developing
labor-saving techniques and processes are an important
element in the essentiality of union labor.   Condition 2
means that consumers should not reduce their purchases of the
final product by a large amount in response to a small increase
in its price.   This condition can be considered at two levels.
If a union has organized all of the firms producing a product
in a particular product market, then the condition refers to
the market for the product as a whole.   It is an advantage to
the union to produce a product for which there are no good
substitutes, for then increases in the product price are not
likely to cause large reductions in the amount consumed.   If
the union has not organized all the firms producing the particular product, then we must consider the demand for the
product of the union firms.   Here the product of the non-
union firms will usually be a very good substitute, so that a
small rise in the price charged by union firms will cause them
to lose a large share of the market.   Empirically, this is
probably the most important implication of the theory.
There have been numerous cases in which the failure of a
union to organize all the firms in a product market has left it
unable to sustain its wage gains or even its very existence.   In
the 1920's, the United Mine Workers made very large wage
gains in unionized coal fields, but these fields soon lost
important markets to the non-union fields, and this led to a
rapid decline in the employment of union members.   More
recently, the union in the hosiery industry has all but disappeared because of similar competition in the product
market from non-union firms.
    To consider condition 3, that the cost of union labor be
a small part of total costs, we return again to the case in
which the union has organized the whole product market.
Suppose that there is a related product which is a reasonably
good substitute for the product of the unionized workers.

Ordinarily, this would tend to put the union in a weak position. However, if the union in question represents workers whose wages are a very small part of total cost, then even a large wage increase will have little effect on the price of the product and hence on the volume of sales and employment. For example, let us suppose that the demand for new houses is so elastic that an increase in price of 1 per cent will decrease the volume of construction by 2 per cent. Suppose also that the wages of electricians make up 1 per cent of the total cost of a new house, and that there are absolutely no substitutes for their services. In this case, an increase in the wages of electricians of 50 per cent would add only one half of 1 per cent to the total price of a house and, despite the high elasticity of demand we have assumed, would reduce the volume of construction by only 1 per cent.[1]

Empirically, the importance of the share of union wages in total cost may lie in the large range of variation in this share among unions. Union wages have at times been as high as two-thirds of total cost in coal mining and can be a small fraction of 1 per cent of total cost for a highly specialized craft union such as pattern-makers. This consideration would lead us to predict that craft unions will in general have more effect than industrial unions on the wages of their members. It should be noted, however, that a craft union has the advantage of being unimportant in total cost only if it bargains as a separate unit, and if unions representing other occupations do not automatically get wage increases as large as those won by the first union. When it becomes certain that increases

[1] In exceptional circumstances, the union is in a better position if it is important in total costs than if it is unimportant. The circumstances are those in which there are relatively good substitutes for union labor in the production process and the demand for the final product is highly inelastic. Here the union has little to fear from raising the price of the final product. If union labor is important, it becomes more difficult for employers to find substitutes for all of it, and the larger the quantities in which they must use the substitutes, the more they drive up their prices. For the original statement of this exception, see J. R. Hicks, *The Theory of Wages* (London: Macmillan and Co., 1935), pp. 241–46.

granted to one craft union will always be extended to the rest, the relevant variable for each union becomes the share of all wages in total cost, and not the share of the wages of its own members. There is no particular reason why the share of all wages in total cost should be smaller for an industry organized on a craft basis than for one organized on an industrial basis.

Condition 4, that the supply of other factors of production be inelastic, means that if the employer tries to economize on union labor by using more of some other factor of production, the price of that factor should rise appreciably in response to his increased use of it. This will be important where condition 1 is not well satisfied.

The elasticity of demand for union labor will limit the wage gains of a union only if the union is concerned about the employment of its members. Of two unions facing identical demand curves, the one most willing to tolerate loss of employment by its members will make the largest wage gains (assuming that the two have equal bargaining skill, and so do the two employers). A union will ordinarily be less concerned about loss of employment among its members where they have good alternative employment opportunities.

Taken together, Marshall's four conditions suggest that there are economic limits imposed on the power of a union to raise wages in a number of different directions. That we do not observe unions with the power to double the wages of their members, or observe them only very rarely and for brief periods, suggests that it is not likely that all the conditions for great union power will be fully satisfied at the same time.

§ 2. Measuring the Impact of the Union. The impact of the union on relative wages has been defined here as the extent to which a union raises the wages of its members and the other workers for whom it bargains above the wages of comparable unorganized workers. This effect can be measured in either of two ways: in cross-section, by comparing the wages of union workers at a point in time with the wages of non-union workers in other occupations or localities, and in time series, by comparing the movement of wages of union workers through time with those of non-union workers. Sometimes the two methods can be combined in a single study. The cross-section method has substantial advantages where wage bargaining takes place in local product markets, some of which are unorganized or only partially organized.

Making useful comparisons is not always easy. If we compare wages in union and non-union plants in the same industry and labor market, we may observe only small differences even where the union is effective, for non-union employers will often be forced to raise wages if they want to prevent the unionization of their workers. Some economists have argued that such considerations vitiate all comparisons between union and non-union wages. This claim, however, is surely too sweeping. A union wage increase will not necessarily affect the wages of non-union workers in other localities or other industries, and if it does have an effect, this effect can be in either direction. In some cases, the union wage increase may be emulated. In others, the effect will operate through the labor market in the opposite direction. The higher wages in the union sector will tend to check the growth of employment in that sector, which will increase the supply of labor to the non-union sector and tend to check increases in non-union wages.

When we begin to make comparisons across localities or industries, new problems arise in defining comparable workers. We would not expect wages in two industries to move in exactly the same way if both were unorganized, for there will be changes through time in the forces governing the size of interindustry wage differentials. Similarly, the wages in the same occupation in two cities will not usually be the same if both are unorganized. There will almost always be some differential whose size is determined by such forces as the age and skill of the workers, the size of the cities, the intensity of the local demand for labor, and the general level of income in the area or region in which the cities are located. In making comparisons between union and non-union wages, there is therefore always a danger of confounding the effect of the union with the effects of other forces that contribute to wage differentials in the absence of unions.   These other forces must be carefully considered, and their effects must in so far as possible be removed from the data by appropriate statistical procedures.   The resulting estimates of union effect cannot be regarded as exact but should give us the rough order of magnitude of the union effect.

§ 3. **Research Findings.**   Research on the impact of the union on wages has proceeded along two lines.   One group of studies has examined a large number of industries simultaneously, classifying them according to the degree of unionization.[1] A second group of studies is based on the intensive examination of the effects of unions on earnings in a single industry.[2] Most of the cross-section studies fall in this group.

Because I shall rely rather heavily in what follows on the estimates made in some of these studies, it is desirable to give some explanation of the estimating techniques that have been used.   To use the time-series technique, one must construct a

[1] See Arthur M. Ross, "The Influence of Unionism upon Earnings," *Quarterly Journal of Economics*, February, 1948; Arthur M. Ross and William Goldner "Factors Affecting the Interindustry Wage Structure," *Quarterly Journal of Economics*, May, 1950; and Harold M. Levinson, *Unionism, Wage Trends, and Income Distribution* (Ann Arbor: University of Michigan Press, 1951).   A new study of this general type is now being conducted by Professor H. Gregg Lewis.   His preliminary results were reported in a paper entitled "The Effects of Unions on Industrial Wage Differentials" presented at Princeton, New Jersey, April, 1960, to a conference on labor economics held by the National Bureau of Economic Research.

[2] See Stephen P. Sobotka, "Union Influence on Wages: The Construction Industry," *Journal of Political Economy*, April, 1953; Joseph Scherer, "The Union Impact on Wages: The Case of the Year-Round Hotel Industry," *Industrial and Labor Relations Review*, January, 1956; Elton Rayack, "The Impact of Unionism on Wages in the Men's Clothing Industry, 1911–1956," *Labor Law Journal*, September, 1958; Melvin Lurie, "The Effect of Unionization on Wages in the Transit Industry," *Journal of Political Economy*, June, 1961; and Rush V. Greenslade, "The Economic Effects of Collective Bargaining in Bituminous Coal Mining," (unpublished Ph.D. dissertation, University of Chicago, 1952).

historical wage series for the unionized group going back far enough to include a period in which it was not unionized. It is also necessary to have a comparison or "base" series, often much broader in scope, showing the movement of wages or earnings for a group of workers who remain unorganized throughout the period of the study, or whose extent of unionization is appreciably less. If the workers of the base group are unorganized throughout, the analysis might proceed as follows: Suppose that in the period before the formation of the union under study, the average ratio of wages in the study group to wages in the base group in years of reasonably full employment was 1.20 to 1 and that in the period after the unionization of the study group this average ratio was 1.40 to 1 in comparable years. The estimate of the relative effect of unions on wages would then be approximately 17 per cent.[1] Before the estimate could be accepted, it would have to be determined whether factors other than unionization might account for changes in the ratio. It might also be possible to attach significance to changes in the ratio during the period of unionization.

The cross-section technique refers to a particular year. It can most easily be described for the case in which it is applied to separate local labor markets, in each of which the group under study can be described as entirely unionized or entirely non-unionized. For each market the wages of workers in the study group are divided by the wages of workers in some common base group in which workers are nowhere extensively unionized, such as retail trade, or in which there is little variation in the extent of unionization from place to place. If the base group is nowhere unionized, the estimate is made as follows: Suppose that the average ratio of wages in the study group to those in the base group is 1.40 to 1 in the unionized cities and 1.20 to 1 in the non-union cities. Then the estimate of the relative wage effect of the union in the year studied is again 17 per cent. The purpose of the use of the

[1] This figure is obtained by dividing 1.40 by 1.20 and subtracting 1.00. The result is then expressed as a percentage by multiplying it by 100.

base group is to eliminate or reduce the effect of differences in wage levels among places that are not the result of unionization.[1]

Having sketched briefly the nature of the research techniques that have been used, I shall now attempt to summarize the findings of this body of research and to make some educated guesses to fill in the gaps. The summary will attempt to indicate both the possible average effect of unions on relative wages, and the range of variation among unions in these effects, though the estimates of the latter kind will be subject to larger errors. Initially, the effects will be stated in terms of the percentage by which unions raise relative earnings in periods of reasonably full employment and reasonably stable prices.

Strong American unions seem to be able to raise the relative earnings of their members by 15 to 25 per cent. Sobotka's study of the skilled building trades unions, as reinterpreted by H. G. Lewis, suggests a figure toward the high end of this range. It seems probable that craft unions in the printing, railroad, and entertainment industries have at times had effects of this general magnitude, though in recent years declines in demand and technological change may be eroding the power of some of them. Some industrial unions also seem to have effects of this order. Greenslade's study indicates that the United Mine Workers had an effect of at least 20 per cent on relative earnings in 1950–51, and Rayack has estimated that the effect of unionization in men's clothing was about 20 per cent in the early 1920's. Although no study of this type has been

[1] If the industry or occupation in question is one in which the extent of unionization varies continuously from one market to another, the cross-section technique can still be used. It will then involve estimating a regression equation in which the dependent variable is the ratio of wages in the study group to wages in the base group, and the independent variable is the percentage of workers in the study group who are organized. Ideally, the measure of union effect as we have defined it is the difference in the level of the regression line at zero and 100 per cent unionization, though this measure is subject to error if, for example, either extreme lies outside the actual range of observations. Readers with no background in statistics may safely ignore this footnote and rely on the text.

made of the teamsters' union, its rapid growth and generally aggressive attitude might lead one to classify it among the strong unions, at least for a large portion of its jurisdiction.

Little research has been done on the effects on earnings of industrial unions in the mass-production manufacturing industries during periods of reasonably stable prices. In the light of what we know about other unions, an effect of 10 to 15 per cent for the strong unions in this group, such as the steelworkers, does not seem unreasonable.

Some recent studies have found periods of stable prices and high employment in which the unions studied had no measurable influence on earnings. The unions for which this was found are of two general types. First, there are those which bargain with firms selling in national product markets and which have failed to organize a substantial majority of the firms in their industry. At the present time, the unions in the textile industry are the best example of this situation. Wage increases in the unionized sector that exceed those in the non-union sector give the non-union firms a competitive advantage in the product market and therefore have large effects on employment in union firms. The union lacks power because the products of non-union labor are an almost perfect substitute for the products of union labor.

There are other cases in which unions have little or no measurable effect on earnings even though they have organized almost all of the firms in their jurisdictions. Two such cases that have been studied are those of the Amalgamated Clothing Workers and the Amalgamated Association of Street Railway and Motor Coach Operators in the period since World War II. Both of these unions had had substantial effects on the earnings of their members in earlier periods. The relevant common factor is that both unions operate in industries where the demand for the final product has been declining in recent years. The resulting declines in employment and the precarious financial position of many employers have apparently made the unions unwilling to risk further losses in employment by an aggressive wage policy. This attitude is reinforced by the effect of declining employment in raising the average age of union members. Older workers are less mobile and have poorer alternatives in the labor market and will therefore be more concerned with saving their jobs than with higher wage rates.

My own best guess of the average effects of all American unions on the wages of their members in recent years would lie somewhere between 10 and 15 per cent. This is within the range of the estimates being made by H. G. Lewis in his current work covering the whole economy, though his results would not rule out an average effect somewhat higher than this.

The preceding discussion has taken conditions of relatively stable prices and relatively full employment as a norm for measuring union effects on relative wages. We must now ask what deviations from these effects occur under other conditions.

In periods of rapid and unexpected inflation, such as occurred from 1941 to 1948, even the strongest unions seem to have no effect on relative earnings, or to lose most of any effect they previously had.[1] During rapid inflations, demand forces pull up product prices and wage rates in non-union markets. Agreements fixing wages for a period of time, or even long-term agreements providing for periodic wage increases according to some preagreed formula or schedule can leave unions at a relative disadvantage. The presence of a union, with its power to resist wage cuts at a later date, can also dissuade employers from using wage increases to deal with temporary labor shortages.

The sluggishness in wage adjustment created by collective bargaining, which acts to a union's disadvantage in periods of very rapid price and wage increases, becomes an advantage in periods of recession or in the early stages of a depression. Here union wages may remain fixed while other wages decline, increasing the union's normal effect on relative wages. Such an effect operated in the building and printing industries from

---

[1] See Sobotka, *op. cit.*, pp. 139–41, Levinson, *op. cit.*, pp. 33–39 and 47–62, and A. Rees, "Postwar Wage Determination in the Basic Steel Industry," *American Economic Review*, June, 1951.

1929 to 1931, as may be seen by comparing their wage movements with those of other industries in which there are a large number of small employers. Because the recessions of the past fifteen years have been comparatively mild, effects of this sort have not been of appreciable importance since 1945. When a depression becomes prolonged and severe, as in 1931–33, the union effect on relative earnings again tends to disappear. Some unions lose their bargaining rights over much of their jurisdictions, some accept wage cuts that wipe out their relative advantages, and still others preserve the union scale, but permit such substantial amounts of work to be done at wages below the scale that the scale becomes largely a fiction. Fortunately, we have had no opportunity to observe how the stronger unionism of today would adjust to severe depression.

§ 4. Non-economic Limits on Union Impact. The rough summary of the literature on union effects in the last section suggests that a 25 per cent effect on relative earnings is a large one, one not often exceeded according to the studies made so far. From two points of view, however, this effect may seem rather small. First, it seems small from the point of view of the casual observer, the "man in the street." His offhand impression may be that unions often double the wages of their members. All of his sources of information are biased in the direction of leading him to guess too high. Newspapers and broadcasters give prominent coverage to wage increases resulting from strike settlements or from large-scale negotiations because they are dramatic, while little attention is paid to the gradual upward creep of non-union wages. Small wonder that the public does not suspect that in this race the tortoise sometimes catches up with the hare. The unions themselves tend to take credit for more than their due. Thus a union paper may say to the members, "In 1939 you were earning 70 cents an hour; today you earn $2.50 an hour. This is what your union has done for you." The average reader will not see that much of this increase is due to the rise in the general price level and the increasing productivity of labor, and would thus have taken place even without the union. It might be thought that employers would seek to deny such excessive union claims, but often they have their own reasons for making similar statements. Employers may exaggerate the union effect on earnings to win support for the position that unions have too much power and should be restrained by public policy.

The rather modest size of measured union effects on relative earnings may also be somewhat surprising from the point of view of economic theory. Surely there are cases where, in the short run at least, the demand for union labor is highly inelastic, so that very substantial increases in relative earnings would have little adverse effect on employment. For some of the highly skilled craft unions, this might be true even over long periods. This suggests that employment effects are not the only force tending to limit the size of union wage gains. Although other possible forces are not dealt with by the received theory, it may be useful to speculate about them.

Workers, employers, and the public undoubtedly have rough ideas about the levels of wages required to get an adequate supply of labor for jobs at various levels of skill. These rough ideas are the basis of the concepts of equity that are so important in explicit discussion of wage differentials. When a union rate is more than about 25 per cent above the non-union level for similar work, it may be viewed by employers or the public as unfair or unreasonable. Such very high rates will often be accompanied by visible job rationing—conditions of unemployment of qualified workers in times of prosperity, or discriminatory or unduly exacting conditions for entry to employment or union membership. These will increase the sense of unfairness. The result may be stiffened employer resistance to wage demands even when business is good and increased public support for employers in time of dispute.

It would be unreasonable to expect the union or its members to perceive their wage as too high. They may, however, perceive it as "high enough" and prefer to avoid strikes rather than raise it still further.   If a union has a high relative wage and still has unexploited bargaining power, it may use this to improve the non-wage conditions of employment.   Since these cannot be measured in a single dimension, they are less likely to attract attention and to arouse resentment.   The union may also try to force the employer to use more labor at the union wage than he would freely choose to employ—that is, it may force him off of his demand curve to the right.   This possibility has been neglected in our earlier discussion, and full discussion of it will be reserved for Chapter VI.   In this context, it is important to note only that it is a way of increasing the income of the membership, assuming that the members have been experiencing some unemployment, without creating a wage that appears unfairly high.

The union studied whose impact on earnings seems to be most in excess of the normal range is the Airline Pilots' Association.   This union meets all of the theoretical criteria for expecting a large effect.   In addition, the responsibility of its members for the lives of their passengers serves to insulate it from adverse public reaction to very high earnings.   If you tell the average airline passenger that the pilot of a large jet aircraft may earn more than $25,000 a year, he is likely to reply, "Well, you can't pay these fellows too much to suit me."   There is, however, no basis for believing that a lower salary would fail to attract enough pilots who were fully qualified in every respect having any bearing on passenger safety.   The unusual features of this exception tend to confirm the rule that unions will ordinarily hesitate to set wages palpably above the levels needed to secure an adequate supply of qualified applicants during periods of full employment.

§5. The Relation between Union Impact and Market Structure.
In the preceding discussion of union impact, nothing was said about the market organization of the industries with which the unions bargain; that is, about whether they are highly competitive or monopolistic in the sale of their products.   Some economists feel that this is a significant variable and that unions

make larger gains when they deal with monopolies because they are able to "capture" some of the monopoly profit arising in the product market. It has even been argued that union power is primarily a response to the power of business monopolies—in Galbraith's terms that it is "countervailing" power rather than "original" power.[1]

It is difficult to find support for this position in fact or in theory. Historically, the first unions organized were in industries where most employers were small firms (the outstanding exceptions are the railroads and anthracite mining). In printing, building construction, entertainment, bituminous coal mining, the local service industries, the garment industries, and similar highly competitive industries, we find most of the large craft and industrial unions of the period before 1933. We also find in these competitive sectors most of the unions shown by recent research to have a large effect on relative earnings, though it must be admitted that much of the research has been concentrated on this sector, in part because it lends itself better to the cross-section study.

It is clear that the great financial resources of large firms in such industries as steel, meat-packing, and automobiles were used to help delay the organization of these industries. These firms used their resources to win strikes and to maintain elaborate spy and police systems that prevented unions from getting a secure foothold before the 1930's. This, however, does not meet the argument that once collective bargaining has been accepted in such an industry the union has a special advantage.

The argument that unions have a special advantage in bargaining with a monopolist rests on two kinds of evidence. The first is the conviction of union leaders and students of the day-to-day operation of collective bargaining that unions make larger gains when dealing with monopolistic industries. The second is that three competent statistical studies show a

[1] See John Kenneth Galbraith, *American Capitalism: A Theory of Countervailing Power* (New York: Houghton Mifflin and Co., 1956), pp. 115 ff.

significant correlation between the extent of concentration in the product market (the best available general measure of monopoly power) and wage increases, and two of the three suggest a further correlation between these two variables and the extent of unionization.[1] All three of these studies, and perhaps the more general impression mentioned above, are based on the experience of manufacturing industries. It does seem to be true that in manufacturing, at least in recent years, the most successful unions have dealt with the concentrated industries, though the printing trades unions are an exception. However, this may be because some of the less successful unions in shoes, textiles, and apparel have been dealing with declining or partially organized industries rather than because they were dealing with competitive industries. Moreover, the generalization does not hold when a broader range of industries is considered. Such highly successful and powerful unions as the United Mine Workers, the teamsters, and the building trades unions deal with industries that are highly competitive, or would be in the absence of unions.

In this discussion, it is important to classify industries as competitive or monopolistic according to their market structure under non-union conditions, since one of the effects of unions in such industries as the building trades and the local service industries may be to create effective cartels in the product market. This possibility is suggested by a number of antitrust cases based on union-employer collusion affecting product prices and the entry of firms into product markets. More study of the nature and importance of such collusion is badly needed.

Professor Melvin W. Reder has pointed out another difficulty encountered by the statistical studies cited above. All of them

[1] See Joseph Garbarino, "A Theory of Interindustry Wage Structure Variation," *Quarterly Journal of Economics*, May, 1950; Harold M. Levinson, *Postwar Movement of Prices and Wages in Manufacturing Industries* ("Study Paper" No. 21, Joint Economic Committee, 86 Cong. 2d sess., 1960); and William G. Bowen, *Wage Behavior in the Postwar Period: An Empirical Analysis* (Industrial Relations Section, Princeton University, 1960).

correlate wage *changes*, rather than wage *levels*, with the extent of monopoly in product markets. On the assumption that monopoly in product markets is conducive to high wages, one would expect wage levels to be related to the extent of monopoly and wage increases to be related to increases in the extent of monopoly, for if an industry is continuously monopolized, why is not this as much an advantage to the union at the beginning of a period as at the end? The correlations reported by Garbarino, Levinson, and Bowen, unless they happen to depend on the particular time periods covered, suggest an ever increasing differential between the wages paid by monopolists and by competitors for comparable labor. Eventually, such a growing differential would become grossly apparent, and it is not.

On theoretical grounds, there is little reason to believe that it is an advantage to the union to bargain with a monopolist. The possibilities for substituting other factors of production for union labor should not differ systematically according to market structure. The principal apparent difference lies in the price adjustment to a cost increase. A competitive industry will eventually pass all of a cost increase on to consumers in higher product prices[1] and will regain its normal rate of return on capital. In the process the size of the industry will be somewhat reduced. The reduction in industry output and employment will restrain the union's original wage demands if it is foreseen, or postpone or moderate future wage demands if it is not.

A monopolized industry, if it maximizes profits both before and after the increase in costs, may not pass on the full amount of the cost increase in prices and the cost increase will lower monopoly profits. Presumably this is what is meant by the statement that unions can "capture" such profits. But this

---

[1] It is assumed in the text that the industry does not use any highly specialized factors of production other than labor. If it does, some of the wage increase could be shifted backward in lower prices for these specialized inputs. Any changes in costs related to the size of the industry are also ignored.

will be an advantage to the union only if the effects of the price
increase on output and employment are smaller for a monopolistic than for a competitive industry. Since the maximizing monopoly may add only a portion of the increased
cost to product prices, this would seem at first glance to be
true. This seeming advantage is offset, however, by the fact
that for given demand and cost conditions the monopoly starts
with a higher price and a smaller output; these are the
necessary consequences of its use of its monopoly power.[1]
At this higher price and smaller output, the demand for the
product will usually be more elastic; that is, a given percentage price increase will cause a larger percentage reduction
in output and employment. This can cancel the advantage to
the union of not having the full cost increase added to prices.[2]

The discussion of the preceding paragraph assumes that the
monopolist maximizes money profits, which is the conventional
assumption of economic theory. However, there are some
plausible models of monopoly behavior that do not involve
this assumption. It would be favorable to the union if after
the wage increase the monopolist were to raise prices by less
than would maximize profits in the long run, but there does
not seem to be any mechanism that would lead to this result
short of government price controls of a kind we have never
had in peacetime. Indeed, the opposite result seems much
more probable—that the monopolist will come closer to

[1] The assumption that a monopolist and a competitive industry can
have identical costs is sometimes questioned on the grounds that the
monopolist will reorganize or "rationalize" the industry. For a statement of this objection, see Joan Robinson, *The Economics of Imperfect
Competition* (London: Macmillan and Co., 1933), Book IV, Chapter XIV.

[2] For a simplified special case it can easily be shown that this offset is exact;
that the percentage decline in output is the same for a monopolistic and a
competitive industry if the two wage increases, and the two demand
curves, and the two cost curves are the same. The case is that in which
the demand curves are straight lines, long-run average costs are constant
over variations in industry output, and the monopolist maximizes in the
long run by equating marginal revenue with long-run average (equals
marginal) cost. Readers who do not understand this note and would
like to should consult an elementary textbook in economic theory.

maximizing profits after the wage increase than before.   In
the period immediately after World War II, when such concentrated industries as steel and automobiles were charging
prices too low to clear the market, negotiated wage increases
were used as an occasion to raise prices by more than the direct
increase in labor cost.   These industries thus took advantage
of collective bargaining to move closer to a profit-maximizing
position, which in itself is unfavorable to the union.[1]

Nevertheless, it may be an advantage for a union to bargain
with an oligopolist when there is excess demand, for if the
oligopoly price fails to clear the market both before and after
the wage increase, the union need not fear reduction in
employment in the short run as a result of reduced consumption of the product.   At the new higher price, production will
still be at full capacity.   In a competitive industry where
product markets are continuously cleared, a higher price will
always have an adverse effect on consumption, at the very least
in causing it to expand at a slower rate.

§ 6. Relative Wages and Resource Allocation.

In the previous
discussion of wages, it has been assumed that union-imposed
increases in relative wages will cause employment to be smaller
than it otherwise would be in the sector covered by the wage
increases.   This assumption, which follows from the principal
propositions of traditional economic theory, deserves more
careful examination than it has been given so far, particularly
since most unionists and many labor economists deny it.

Let me begin by emphasizing again that the theory does not
predict absolute declines in employment wherever unions raise
relative wages.   If unions raise relative wages in a rapidly
growing industry or firm, employment will usually continue
to grow, but not as much as it would have otherwise.   Several
elaborate attempts to measure the employment effect of wage
increases have been inadequate because of confusion on this
point.   Second, employment should for this purpose be

[1] See A. Rees, "Wage-Price Relations in the Basic Steel Industry,"
Industrial and Labour Relations Review, January, 1953.

measured in man-hours and not in men, though for convenience we have been talking about it as though it were
always measured in men. A union faced with an employer
decision to cut labor input in response to a wage increase can
sometimes choose to spread the work in the form of shorter
hours rather than to accept layoffs. The prediction does not
depend on any one line of response to the increase in relative
wages. In some instances the employment effect will operate
largely by stimulating the introduction of labor-saving
machinery, in some by reducing the sales of the final product,
in still others by less obvious kinds of substitutions. It is not
even necessary that any employer make a conscious adjustment to the higher wages, provided that the different employers
affected start with different proportions of wages to total cost.
Under these circumstances, the employers with the smallest
proportion of wages to total cost will tend to grow relative to
the others because their cost structure has an improved survival
value under the changed conditions, and this will tend to
reduce the input of labor in the industry as a whole relative to
what it would otherwise have been.[1]

The most frequent objection to this theory has been that
wage increases improve efficiency, and the greater efficiency
makes it unnecessary to reduce employment. Sometimes the
introduction of labor-saving machinery is cited as an example
of such improved efficiency. Here two cases must be distinguished. The first is that in which the new machinery would
have been unprofitable before the wage increase but is profitable afterward. In this case the total costs of production will
rise, though the rise will be smaller than if methods of production had remained unchanged. The higher total costs will
ordinarily be reflected in product prices, so that employment
is reduced both by the change in production methods and by
the decreased sales of the product. The guarantee that costs
rise in this case is of course contained in the statement that the
machinery was unprofitable before the wage increases. Since

[1] See Armen Alchian, "Uncertainty, Evolution, and Economic Theory,"
Journal of Political Economy, June, 1950.

this case is clearly part and parcel of the original argument for an employment effect, it is surprising to find it cited in rebuttal.

A rather similar line of argument points out that union wage increases will tend to eliminate the least efficient firms, and that this will cause employment to grow in the remaining, more efficient firms.   This may indeed result, but it is highly unlikely that the growth of employment in the remaining firms would offset the decline in employment in those that disappear, particularly since the remaining firms will tend to be those that use the least labor per unit of output.

What critics of the theory probably have in mind is the second case, in which the machinery would have been profitable even before the wage increase but the employers did not realize it.   In seeking to adjust to the wage increase, they discover their neglected opportunities.   In this case total costs and prices could be lower after the wage increase than before, and the larger sales of the product could offset the adverse effect on employment of the change in methods of production. This is one variety of the so-called "shock effect" argument. The argument can turn on improved personnel practices, changes in hiring standards, or reduction of wastes of various sorts rather than on the introduction of new equipment.

Controversy over the shock effect centers on its importance rather than its logical consistency.   It can certainly be conceded that few organizations operate continuously at peak efficiency, and that an occasional jolt or crisis can help to bring a firm closer to its best performance level.   It may also be conceded that wage increases are probably more effective in helping to improve the efficiency of personnel management or production techniques than are shocks from more remote areas of the firm's operation, such as the introduction of an improved product by a competitor.   Such challenges are most likely to be met in kind—product redesign by product redesign, price cut by price cut, and so on.   But this is not sufficient to establish the importance of the shock effect.   The degree of inefficiency prior to the wage increase must be very large indeed if the effects of eliminating it will more than offset the entire cost of the wage increase, so that product prices actually fall and sales increase enough to absorb the labor displaced by the more efficient methods. Such large shock effects may be plausible in a few cases where unions are newly established. But it is not plausible to expect them repeatedly as the union wins subsequent wage increases. A gradual upward union push of relative wages seems no more likely to improve efficiency than any of the many other pressures on a firm in a competitive economy.

It should also be noted, as H. Gregg Lewis has pointed out to me, that the shock-effect argument is inconsistent with the observation that unions seek to equalize wages among firms. If union wage increases have such favorable effects on efficiency that unit costs are not raised, then union wage gains should never put a firm at a disadvantage relative to a non-union competitor. The experience of the coal, textile, and hosiery industries, to name but a few conspicuous cases, contradicts this expectation.

There is unfortunately little direct evidence from research on the employment effects of union wage gains. Rayack finds a sharp reduction in the market shares of output and employment of unionized markets in the men's clothing industry in the years 1923-29.[1] Sobotka reports a statistically significant negative correlation for 1939 between the degree of union organization of skilled building trades workers by cities and the ratio of months worked per year between such workers and a base group of non-union workers in the same cities.[2] There is also a careful study of the employment effects of minimum wage laws that finds substantial and consistent effects.[3] The traditional theory and the objections to the

[1] *Op. cit.*, p. 682.
[2] *Op. cit.*, p. 137.
[3] John M. Peterson, "Employment Effects of Minimum Wages, 1938–1950," *Journal of Political Economy*, October, 1957, and "Employment Effects of State Minimum Wages for Women: Three Historical Cases Re-examined," *Industrial and Labor Relations Review*, April, 1959. See also the comment by Richard A. Lester on these articles and the reply by Peterson, *ibid.*, January, 1960.

theory are the same for legally imposed minimum wages as they are for union-won wage increases.

Apart from the rather scanty published research bearing on this issue, there is at least one important case, that of bituminous coal, in which employment effects seem obvious to casual observation. The United Mine Workers has been mentioned earlier as a union with substantial effects on relative wages operating in an industry in which employment has declined sharply. The recent shifts in demand for bituminous coal have been of a kind that would probably have occurred to almost the same extent in the absence of union wage increases. The crucial point, however, is that there has been a drastic reduction in the amount of labor used to produce a given output. While some of this represents autonomous improvements in technology and some may be the result of shifts in the composition of output by uses, most of it seems to represent the rapid extension, in response to the rising wage, of long-known techniques for saving labor by the increased use of capital. Types of mining that use little labor, such as strip mining, have expanded rapidly even though the union has in effect discriminated against them by financing its generous health and welfare program by a tonnage royalty on output rather than by the usual contribution based on payrolls.

Before we leave the discussion of employment effects, we should consider a special case in which economic theory does not necessarily predict a fall in employment as the result of unionization and the imposition of a union wage scale. This is the case of monopoly in the hiring of labor, usually called labor monopsony. Let us consider first the case of the employer who is the sole user of a certain kind of labor in his labor market. He will find that as he increases his use of this kind of labor, he must raise his wages to attract enough qualified workers. (The same is true of employers as a group in a competitive labor market, but the individual employer in such a market can hire more labor at the going wage.) Our monopsonistic employer will be restrained from expanding employment by the fact that the cost of new employees consists not only of their own wage, but also of the wage increases that must be given to the old employees.[1]   If a union now imposes a standard wage slightly above the wage previously paid, the employer finds that the cost of each new worker consists of his own wage alone, and this tends to induce him to employ more workers at the union wage than he employed previously.   If the union wage is high enough, this effect will disappear and the ordinary adverse effect of wage increases on employment will reassert itself.

The kind of monopsony considered in the preceding example grows out of the concentration of employment in an area in one employer or a very small number of employers.   Such employer concentration is not common in the United States, though it exists in some textile and mining towns.[2]   It has probably diminished substantially in recent years as the wide-spread ownership of cars by industrial workers and the improvement of highways have extended the effective com-muting radius to fifty miles or more and have facilitated the permanent movement of labor.

A second kind of monopsony is also possible, that caused by collusive agreement among the employers in an area.   Such agreements can set ceilings on wages or wage increases, or more commonly can ban the "pirating" of labor—the hiring of workers already employed in the area without the consent of their present employer.   When there is an ample supply of labor in a market, there is usually no need for any such agree-ments, and when the market is very tight, there is grave doubt that they are effective or enforceable.   The anti-pirating agreement can be evaded by workers by the simple expedient of quitting their jobs, which in a tight labor market involves little risk.   The firm can evade a maximum wage agreement by

[1] In the usual terminology of the theory, the marginal labor cost exceeds the wage.   The argument does not apply, of course, if the employer can successfully pay lower wages to his original workers than to new workers of the same ability, but such cases must be extremely rare for manual labor.

[2] Estimates of employer concentration have been made by Robert Bunting in an unpublished Ph.D. dissertation, University of Chicago.

lowering its hiring standards and thus making a concealed increase in its wage for new workers. Perhaps collusive monopsony has some impact in labor markets moving from looseness to tightness; perhaps it is largely a ceremony by which the personnel directors of expanding firms avoid giving offense to their colleagues in other firms.

Those labor economists who believe strongly in the importance of shock effects and who see the American labor market as shot through with monopsony do not believe that unions as a whole have adverse effects on the allocation of labor. Most economists, however, would agree that unions, in so far as they have the power to raise relative wages, reduce employment in the union sector and increase it in the non-union sector. This is a worse allocation of labor than would exist without unions, in the sense that a shift of labor toward the union sector could increase the total output of the economy. In the union situation, the same individual might be able to earn $2.00 an hour in non-union employment and $2.20 in union employment, and he might be entirely willing to make the shift if jobs were available in the union sector. That this situation reduces the national output follows from viewing the wage as a measure of what the worker is worth to the employer and to the economy. The union employer is not willing to add another man at $2.20 because the man would not contribute that much to the value of production, but there would usually be some wage just below the union wage at which the worker would be hired and at which he would still be willing to shift. The difference between this wage and the wage in the non-union sector after he has shifted is the measure of the loss in output from having him in the wrong place. In the absence of the union, as more workers shifted the wage differential would tend to disappear, along with the potential gain in output from further reallocation.

The preceding argument does not assume that without unions the mobility of labor would be perfect and everyone would work where he gets the highest income and contributes the most to the national product. Income is not always a good measure of the value of a man's contribution to society, and there are substantial interferences with the optimum allocation of labor quite apart from unions. Perhaps the most important of these is the lack of good information about alternative jobs. The argument only states that the union impact on relative wages adds to these interferences rather than subtracts from them. The orthodox economist does not view the disturbance in allocation created by unions as like the effect of throwing a stone into the glassy surface of a pond, for no such glassy surface ever existed in a real labor market. Rather it is like putting an additional set of snags in a sluggish stream.

The view that unions make for a worse allocation of labor does not necessarily imply an unfavorable judgment of the total effect of unions. There are many other aspects of union activity yet to be considered, and an economy has other and perhaps even more important goals than the most efficient allocation of resources.

§ 7. **The Union Influence on Labor's Share.** Many people view trade unions as a device for increasing the worker's share in the distribution of income at the expense of capital; that is, at the expense of the receivers of rent, interest, and profits. Attempts to test this view, which is often expressed by the unions themselves, have led to a number of studies of the effect of unions on labor's share. The studies to date must be regarded as highly inconclusive; no union effect on labor's share can be discovered with any consistency.[1] The ratio of wages and salaries to national income has been rising steadily for a long time. This rise, however, largely reflects the shift of labor from unincorporated business, especially farms

[1] For a summary of this literature, see Clark Kerr, "Labor's Income Share and the Labor Movement" in G. W. Taylor and F. C. Pierson (eds.), *New Concepts in Wage Determination* (New York: McGraw-Hill Book Co., 1957). For a careful recent study that finds no significant union effect see Norman J. Simler, *The Impact of Unionism on Wage-Income Ratios in the Manufacturing Sector of the Economy* (Minneapolis: University of Minnesota Press, 1961).

(where the labor of the owners or operators is compensated by what appears in the national accounts as profits), to corporate enterprise where all labor is paid by wages and salaries. The statistical adjustments needed to convert the original figures into estimates of the total labor share, including the share of owner labor, are difficult and the results of different procedures do not usually agree. However, all have the effect of reducing the rise in labor's share and leaving a remainder that shows no particular relation to union power.[1]

It may seem very strange that statistical studies can find a considerable effect of unions on wages and none on labor's share. On further consideration, however, this result is quite reasonable. First, the global studies of labor's share cover all the workers in the economy, including the self-employed. Only about one-fourth of this total labor force consists of union members, and some of these are in unions too weak to raise the relative earnings of their members. Even if effective unions raise labor's share in their own industries, the effect would be highly diluted and thus difficult to observe when spread over the whole economy. Second, just as we assume that changes in wages can affect capital's share, so we must recognize that disturbances in the rewards to capital will affect labor's share. An obvious example of this is the rise of labor's share during depressions as a direct result of the fall in profits. These independent changes in the reward to capital again tend to obscure any effects of unions on labor's share. By far the most fundamental point, however, is that a successful union will not necessarily raise labor's share even in its own industry. The wage bill will rise following a wage increase if the demand for labor is inelastic (that is, if the percentage reduction in

[1] See D. Gale Johnson, "The Functional Distribution of Income in the United States, 1850–1952," *Review of Economics and Statistics*, May, 1954. Johnson finds an increase in labor's functional share of national income from about 68 per cent in 1890 to about 75 per cent in 1952 but notes that almost half of the increase was achieved before 1929, while unions were still weak. See also Irving Kravis, "Relative Income Shares in Fact and Theory," *American Economic Review*, December, 1959.

employment is smaller than the percentage increase in wages) and this will raise labor's share in the short run. But as time passes the employer will tend to substitute capital for labor, as we have seen in the case of the coal industry. The price of capital to a particular industry will not usually decline as more of it is used, so that the total payments to capital may rise by more than the rise in the wage bill. In extreme cases, total wage payments may fall as employment contracts so that they are smaller than they were before the wage increase. (In other words, the long-run demand for wage-earner labor may be elastic in certain industries.) It is thus entirely possible for a union simultaneously to raise the relative wages of its members and to reduce their aggregate share of income arising in their industry.

If we have no evidence that the union's gains have generally been made at the expense of capital, we may ask from whom they have been made. One answer has been suggested in the preceding section; they may be made in large part at the expense of non-union labor. That is, the likeliest effect of unions on the distribution of income is to redistribute it among workers. In real terms, this redistribution can be thought of as arising in either or both or two ways: first, the money wages of non-union workers may be held down by the reallocation of labor produced by unionism; second, the non-union workers may have to pay more for the products produced by union labor. The union reply to this position is that non-union workers should organize. But even if all workers were organized into unions, it does not follow that union gains would all be at the expense of capital. It would still be possible for strong unions to make gains at the expense of weak ones, and under a decentralized system of collective bargaining, they undoubtedly would.

§ 8. The Union Influence on the Size Distribution of Income.

People are interested in the functional distribution of income (its division between capital and labor) in part because they believe it to be related to the size distribution, the share of income going to people at different income levels. Most people would like to see this size distribution become more equal, at least to the extent of improving the lot of those at the very bottom. The simplest view of the relation between the two distributions is that workers are poor and the receivers of property income are rich. A union that can raise labor's share can then be viewed as a latter-day version of Robin Hood's merry men, with their headquarters removed from Sherwood Forest to a storefront opposite the mill.

Of course, this view of income distribution is much too simple. In fact, there are relatively few employed manual workers at the bottom of the income distribution. Of the 8.7 million families with 1957 incomes under $2,500, only 1.5 million were headed by employed craftsmen, operatives, or non-farm laborers—that is by people in the major occupation groups strongly organized by unions. Perhaps in the absence of unions this number would be somewhat larger, but it seems clear that low wages are no longer a principal cause of poverty, if they ever were. Almost half of these low income families had heads who were not employed in 1957, and many of these had aged heads, presumably retired.[1] Because large numbers of retired people depend on rents, interest, and dividends for much of their income, it seems probable that income from capital is more important at the very bottom of the income distribution than anywhere else except at the very top.

The union influence on relative earnings implies an influence on the size distribution of income even if there is none on the functional distribution, provided only that the members of effective unions are not equally distributed throughout the size distribution. But this proviso is clearly met, for manual workers are highly concentrated in the middle ranges of the income distribution. To get some idea of the probable union effect on the size distribution, we must look in some detail

[1] The statistics in this paragraph are from Robert J. Lampman, *The Low Income Population and Economic Growth* ("Study Paper" No. 12, Joint Economic Committee, 86 Cong. 1st sess.).

at the income position of the occupations represented by effective unions.

For 1949, the median wage and salary incomes for 118 rather detailed male occupations have been arranged by Miller in deciles based on the number of workers in each occupation.[1] Occupations in which most workers are union members appear throughout the distribution. However, the top deciles of the distribution contain a large number of skilled craft occupations of the kind for which both theory and empirical research suggest that unions have the greatest influence on earnings. The top decile contains railroad conductors, compositors, locomotive engineers, and printing craftsmen other than compositors. The other occupations in this decile are all managerial, professional, or supervisory. The second highest decile contains brakemen, structural metal workers, plumbers, locomotive firemen, electricians, boilermakers, telegraph operators, and (rather surprisingly) baggagemen, express messengers, and railway mail clerks. The highest ranking occupation organized by an industrial union appears in the third decile from the top: operatives, motor vehicle. In all these occupations, the median income from wages and salaries alone is far above the median income from all sources of all males with income in 1949; it is also above the median income from all sources of all white, non-farm males with income, in most cases substantially so. It is true, however, that within these high-income manual occupations the dispersion of income is rather small, so that few manual workers get into the highest income brackets. For example, only 0.2 per cent of locomotive engineers had wage and salary income in 1949 of $10,000 and over, as compared with 17.9 per cent of managers and officials, manufacturing.

Perhaps the best summary statement that can be made from the available evidence about the effect of unions on the size distribution of income is that unions have probably raised many higher income workers from an initial position somewhat

[1] Herman P. Miller, *Income of the American People* (New York: John Wiley and Sons, Inc., 1955), pp. 55–58 and 173–77.

above the middle of the income distribution to a present position closer to the top. They have narrowed the gap between the best paid manual workers and the very rich, and widened the gap between these workers and the very poor. This effect cannot be completely described by calling it either an increase or a decrease in the equality of income distribution, though it seems closer to the latter than to the former.

CHAPTER V

UNIONS AND THE GENERAL LEVEL OF WAGES AND PRICES

§ 1. The Hypothesis of the Wage-Price Spiral. In recent years, the dominant view of the inflationary process has been that it is caused by a wage-price spiral; that we have been experiencing "wage-push" or "cost-push" inflation in which trade unions have played a central role. This chapter will argue a contrary position.

What is meant here by inflation is simply a sustained upward movement in the broad indexes of the prices of final products, of which the best known is the Consumer Price Index of the Bureau of Labor Statistics. Products are defined to include consumer services such as medical care and entertainment. It should be noted that a rise in the level of wages or materials prices is not considered as inflation on this definition provided that it is offset by increased efficiency in the use of labor and materials so that the price level of final products does not rise.

Although our measures of the price level are good and constantly improving, it should not be supposed that they are perfect. The construction of price indexes involves many difficult and perhaps insoluble problems, particularly that of dealing with changes in the quality of products. There is strong reason to believe that some of the measured price rise of recent years represents quality improvement in the goods priced, and that if an index could be devised to allow for this more fully, it would show less inflation than our present indexes.

The hypothesis of the wage-price spiral states that inflation is initiated by wage increases that exceed the rise in average output per man-hour in the economy as a whole. The wage increases are attempts by workers through their unions to raise their standard of living. But wage increases that exceed the growth of productivity mean higher unit labor costs, and these cause producers to raise the prices of products. This defeats the unions' attempt to improve living standards, and they respond with new wage demands. An endless spiral is generated, each step causing the next.

As a description of one sequence of events that takes place during an inflation, the concept of the wage-price spiral is valid and graphic. However, the view that wage increases play a crucial causal or initiating role in the inflationary process is not so obviously correct as it may seem.

The hypothesis of the wage-price spiral was first put forward in newspaper editorials and the speeches of businessmen. Before World War II most economists agreed that inflation was essentially a monetary phenomenon and occurred when at full employment the quantity of money increased faster than the output of the economy. In the past few years, however, many economists have come to accept the spiral hypothesis. In general, they have modified it and made it more complicated than the naïve account given above. They have recognized that for the price level to rise, the quantity of money must rise more rapidly than output, or the rate at which a given amount of money changes hands (the velocity of circulation) must increase. If neither of these things happens, people will not be able to pay the higher prices asked by producers, and the increases in costs will have an adverse effect on employment in the union sector. This will tend to choke off the spiral. Sophisticated versions of the spiral hypothesis therefore add a mechanism by which higher wage and price levels generate an increase in the money supply or in the velocity of circulation, or by which higher wage levels induce the monetary authorities (the government and the central bank) to increase the money supply so as to avert unemployment. This version of the hypothesis is logically consistent. Our task is to see whether it is empirically relevant to recent American inflation.

§ 2. Unions and the Level of Costs. We have seen in Chapter IV that there is a good deal of evidence from research to support the common-sense view that unions can raise the relative earnings of their members. However, we have also seen something less obvious: that unions tend to lose ground in relative wages, or at least not to gain new ground, during very rapid inflations, when the rigidities introduced by collective agreements act as a brake on the upward pull of demand on wages. It follows from this that union wage pressures were not a cause of the rapid inflations accompanying World War II and the Korean War. However, few economists have contended that these inflations were caused by a wage-price spiral, though some might argue that wage-setting mechanisms aggravated the inflationary process. It is generally agreed that the basic cause of these wartime inflations was the rapid increase in demand caused by the wars and by the way in which they were financed—large government deficits covered by borrowing newly created money from the banks. The sophisticated versions of the wage-price spiral hypothesis apply largely to the slower inflation since 1953, the so-called creeping inflation.

From 1953 to 1960 the Consumer Price Index rose 10.6 per cent (annual averages), a rise of 1.5 per cent a year. To try to discover whether unions could have been responsible for this rise, we need to work from the findings about relative wages toward some quantitative notion of the aggregate effect of unions on wages. This notion will necessarily be rough but should be of the right order of magnitude. Let us at first make the assumption, which will be reconsidered shortly, that the relative wage gains of unions come about entirely through increases in the absolute level of union wages and that there is no effect either upward or downward on the wages of non-union workers as a whole. In Chapter IV, a rough estimate or educated guess was made that the average effect of unions on the relative earnings of their members was in the range of 10 to 15 per cent. To reduce this to a single figure, let us use the midpoint of this range, $12\frac{1}{2}$ per cent, as an estimate of union wage effects in 1960.

Union membership is about one-third of the number of wage and salary employees in the economy. Since effective unions are concentrated among the higher-paid wage-earners, we might guess that the wages and wage supplements of organized workers are as much as 40 per cent of the total of wages, salaries, and supplements to wages and salaries in the economy. Wages, salaries, and supplements in turn make up about 70 per cent of total costs of all kinds. On the assumption we have been making, the direct union wage effect on aggregate costs is in the neighborhood of 4 per cent of the total costs of the economy ($.125 \times .40 \times .70 = .035$).

This calculation in itself does not help us much, for we are trying to explain inflation, which is the increase of prices through time, whereas the calculation has given us a rough estimate of union effect at an instant in time. If we assume that unions have always had this much effect, then they have contributed nothing to inflation, even though they may have lowered the output of the economy. To contribute to inflation, the union impact on cost must be increasing.

We know, of course, that the union effect on relative wages does not increase without limit. The research studies discussed earlier suggest that after about a 25 per cent effect, unions must work hard merely to hold their past gains against the encroachment of non-union labor, shifts in the pattern of final demand, and the use of labor-saving processes and materials. But we also know that in periods of rapid inflation the union effect on relative wages is reduced, and the years 1950–52 were such a period. Let us assume that by 1952 the average union effect on earnings had been so eroded that it was only 6 per cent; that about half of our roughly estimated total effect of unions on costs in 1960 has been gained since 1952. The unions would then have raised aggregate costs since 1952 by about

2 per cent.   However, the rate of increase in the Consumer Price Index over the period 1953–60 was 1.5 per cent *a year*, or 10.6 per cent in all.   Hence direct union effects on wage costs, on what seems a generous estimate, account for less than one-fifth of the rise in final prices.

The view that the direct wage effects of unions have played only a small part in recent price rises is further supported by the pattern of price increases since 1953.   The largest increases by far have been in the prices of services.   Though labor is a large part of the cost of services, very few service workers are organized into unions.   The retail price levels of consumer durables, produced though not distributed in highly unionized industries, was almost the same in 1959 as in 1953.[1]

The somewhat speculative argument of this section is not intended to prove that unions cannot cause inflation.   Rather, it is intended to emphasize the crucial role of the impact of union wage effects on non-union wages and other costs. Unions can have a major role in inflation if and only if their effects on wages spread beyond the area of direct union influence and become part of some dynamic process affecting the whole economy.   It is to this possibility that we turn next.

§ 3. The Transmission of Union Wage Gains.   Increases in wages won by unions often have some direct upward impact on the wages of immediately adjacent non-union workers. For example, a firm that agrees to a wage increase for its unionized production workers will often give a similar increase to its non-union clerical employees, both to preserve what seems to be an equitable relation between clerical and manual earnings and to forestall the unionization of its clerical work force.   Similarly, the non-union employers of manual labor in a highly unionized industry will ordinarily grant wage increases whenever increases are won by the union in the industry in order to remove the temptation for their workers

[1] For a more detailed analysis along these lines, see Richard T. Selden, "Cost-Push versus Demand-Pull Inflation," *Journal of Political Economy*, February, 1959.

to join the union. In a less exact way, non-union employers in a wide variety of industries may sometimes be forced to match wage increases won by a dominant union in such heavily unionized labor markets as Akron, Pittsburgh, and Detroit.

These cases might be thought to demonstrate that the influence of unions on wages spreads quite widely beyond the direct area of union organization. One must beware, however, of assuming that in all these cases the non-union workers would not have received their wage increases except for contagion from their unionized neighbors. In recent years the market for clerical workers has often been tighter than the market for manual workers. In several big cities for which data are available, wages in clerical occupations have risen more rapidly than average hourly earnings in manufacturing in the same cities, despite the fact that most manufacturing workers and few clerical workers in these cities are organized. In these circumstances, the clerical employees of firms whose production workers are organized do not necessarily receive larger wage increases because of their proximity to union influence. Rather they receive increases in a different time pattern—in the step-like pattern characteristic of collective bargaining rather than in the gently sloping pattern of unorganized markets. It is often probable that the clerical employees get the wage increases of the union workers and, at other times, additional increases on an individual basis because of labor market pressures. Such cases would be clear evidence that the union influence is confined to timing.

In general, it seems reasonable to believe that in periods of labor shortage, there is considerable union influence on the timing of non-union wage changes and little on their amount. On the other hand, in periods of ample labor supply, only those non-union workers in the immediate vicinity of a union wage increase will benefit from it. They will, for non-market reasons, get wage increases that they otherwise would not have gotten. The effect outside the immediate vicinity will be in the opposite direction. The union wage increase will check the growth of employment in the union sector and its immediate vicinity. It will increase the supply of labor or the surplus of labor in the rest of the non-union sector, and will thus tend to delay or reduce the rise in wages in the non-union sector as a whole.

In some areas of the economy where there is no union organization and little possibility of any in the foreseeable future, the effect of unions must always operate through the labor market. These include domestic service and agriculture, where for the most part income levels are enough lower than in the rest of the economy so that there is always an incentive for labor to leave them when jobs are available in the industrial sectors. To the extent that unions limit the growth of employment in industry, they reduce the flow of labor out of these low-income sectors and reduce the return to the labor that remains. From the point of view of resource allocation this is an undesirable effect, but it is one that lowers rather than raises the general level of labor incomes (wages and incomes from self-employment).

If the extent to which union wage increases are transmitted into the non-union sector and the direction of the net effect on non-union wages as a whole are heavily dependent on the tightness of labor markets, then they are ultimately dependent on the level of aggregate demand in the economy and can be influenced by monetary and fiscal policy. The presence of strong unions in a sector of the economy cannot be said to create a situation in which the general level of wages and labor costs is determined by the institutional arrangements of collective bargaining and is immune from the influence of demand forces. When we consider also that the strength of demand is an important influence on the size of wage increases within the union sector, it can be argued with some force that aggregate demand is still the crucial determinant of the general level of money wages.

It is often argued that monetary and fiscal restraint can check a rise in the general level of wages only by creating unemployment. Since unemployment beyond some frictional level is a greater evil than mild inflation, there would be little support for checking wage increases by deliberately creating unemployment, and unions could still be said to control the general level of wages for all practical purposes. I have myself argued on earlier occasions that union wage pressures will lead to aggregate unemployment in the absence of sufficient demand. This argument would be correct in a static economy in which wages were rigid downward even in the non-union sector. The argument presupposes that there is no autonomous rise in wages in the non-union sector. When this supposition is made explicit, it can be seen that the argument does not fit the facts of American economic growth. There is an autonomous upward trend of wages in the non-union sector created by technical progress in the absence of a falling price level. Any net transfer of labor to the non-union sector arising from the policies of particular unions would act first to reduce this autonomous wage rise. The transfer would have to be very large before it created persistent unemployment by putting downward pressure on a rigid wage floor in the non-union sector. In the absence of adequate demand, the consequences of effective unions for aggregate employment must be largely to perpetuate underemployment, not to create open unemployment (except of a transitional kind). The underemployment takes the form of having too much labor in low productivity occupations like domestic service and the low-income parts of the agricultural economy.

The more closely we examine the effects of strong unions in a sector of the economy on the general level of wages and employment, the more the alleged effects appear to be in fact effects on relative wages and the distribution of employment, and not effects on the economy-wide aggregates at all.

§ 4. Wage-Price Relations. By definition, wage increases in the union sector that exceed the increase in output per man-hour will raise unit labor costs. Up to this point it has been assumed that these higher unit labor costs will be reflected in higher product prices. This assumption is correct in a long-run analysis, for labor costs are a major element in total cost and in the long run prices must cover costs. In the short period, however, the relationships between costs and prices can be quite loose. If costs rise in a competitive industry with stable demand, excess capacity will be created and will prevent price rises from reflecting the cost increase fully until it is eliminated. This may take some time to accomplish.

In a monopolistic industry, cost increases will quickly be passed on in higher prices if demand is high and rising, and may be absorbed for considerable periods if demand is weak or falling. Since World War II many industries dominated by large firms have repeatedly made substantial price increases right after negotiating wage increases. This had tended to create the impression that price increases were the inevitable result of higher labor costs. In fact the industries concerned, of which steel is the most important, have had considerable discretionary control of the amount and timing of price increases. In a period of strong demand for their products and of rises in costs other than the costs of wage labor, they would undoubtedly have chosen to raise prices even in the absence of collective bargaining. Price increases in these circumstances usually serve a useful purpose for the economy in helping to allocate scarce commodities to their most urgent uses. The close linking in time between price increases and wage increases has been a kind of lightning rod, grounding the criticism that struck from all sides at price increases on other occasions. The pattern of timing of price changes directed blame toward the unions for price rises that were often larger than the direct increases in unit labor costs. Given an atmosphere in which the government and the public do not accept increases in demand as legitimate grounds for raising prices, this pricing behavior on the part of large companies is a form of elementary self-defense for which they can hardly be blamed. However, it has created a greatly exaggerated impression of the role of unions in an inflationary process.

In general, a period of rising aggregate demand is one in which increases in labor costs are fully and promptly reflected in product prices, while a period of falling aggregate demand is one in which any increases in costs tend to be absorbed, at least temporarily and in part. This reinforces the view based on labor market conditions that the institutional arrangements of the present American economy do not insulate the general price level from demand forces.

§ 5. The Direct Union Influence on Monetary Policy. The sophisticated versions of the wage-price spiral argument recognize, as we have seen, the need for some way of financing a higher level of wages and prices. Several mechanisms have been proposed by which wage increases in the union sector might be supposed to be self-financing. Higher wages usually require higher payrolls, at least in the short run. Higher wages may also induce investment in labor-saving equipment. If for these reasons employers borrow money from banks or use their cash balances more actively, this could increase the quantity of money or its velocity of circulation. The effect by way of investment assumes that the incentive to invest created by the higher relative cost of labor outweighs the discouraging effect on investment of higher costs in general, and this is by no means certain. Another channel of this general type has sometimes been suggested—the higher level of wages and prices requires higher investment in inventories. Since, however, it is the money value of inventories and not their physical size that changes, the increase in value is self-financing unless old inventories are sold at the old prices. In other words, marking up the prices of existing inventories furnishes the added revenue needed to replace them.

Any mechanism of the sort just discussed assumes a passive monetary policy; the banks must be allowed to expand loans in response to the demands of their borrowers without hindrance from the central bank. Moreover, it is assumed that the central bank does not offset any autonomous changes in velocity that it feels to be undesirable. If wage increases are to generate their own increase in the money supply, the central bank must somehow be induced to permit them to do so.

One way in which the central bank could be forced to permit the increases in the money supply needed to support a higher level of wages and prices would be to have it committed to maintain full employment, defined in some rigid and rigorous way. The United States has had a commitment to maintaining high levels of employment, formally expressed in the Employment Act of 1946 and reinforced by the realization of both major political parties when they have been in power that the electorate will blame an incumbent administration for tolerating excessive unemployment. However, the level of unemployment that has been permitted under this commitment has been a moderately high one. The average unemployment rate during the eight years 1953–60 inclusive was 4.9 per cent of the civilian labor force. When faced with a combination of gently rising prices and fairly high levels of unemployment, the central bank has seemed, both in its pronouncements and in its behavior, to be more concerned with rising prices than with unemployment. To the extent that the price rise under such conditions has been real rather than the result of errors in measurement, it cannot have been the result of any general scarcity of labor, though it could have been in part the result of scarcities of particular kinds of labor and of other specific resources.

Trade unions have been among the most vigorous critics of tight monetary policy and among the most prominent advocates of a more rigorous guarantee of full employment. The policies they supported would probably have reduced unemployment and would have increased the rate of price rise. But the crucial point is that these policies were not in fact followed.

On the other hand, it can be argued that trade unions were an important part of the complex of social and political change of the past thirty years that led to even a weak commitment to the goal of full employment, and that without unions and the political leaders they have supported public policy would have given even higher priority to price stability, with the result that the postwar price rises would have been smaller and the levels of unemployment higher than they have been. In particular, unions may help to create an atmosphere in which downward inflexibility of the price level is widely accepted, so that any increases in prices that occur are allowed to persist and public policy never attempts to "roll back" prices to earlier and lower levels. This point will be discussed in the following section.

§ 6. **Wage and Price Levels during Recessions.** The period since World War II has not been unusual in having rising prices during cyclical expansions in business activity. It has been somewhat unusual in the very small size of general price declines during recessions and in the absence of any decline, according to conventional measures, during the recession of 1958. It has been suggested that union wage pressures are a major cause of this downward rigidity of prices. In other words, unions raise the general level of prices not by making it rise faster than it otherwise would during periods of prosperity, but by preventing it from falling during recessions so as to offset the preceding rises. This view has a good deal to commend it. Unions add to downward wage rigidity and in recent years, through the automatic wage increases provided for in long-term contracts, they have contributed to an unusual rise in average hourly money earnings during cyclical contractions. At the same time it must be recognized that unionization is only one of several forces contributing to this new pattern of wage-price behavior in recessions, and that it is not necessarily the most important one.

The salient feature of postwar recessions from this point of view is that they have been relatively mild and their length from peak to trough has been short. In mild, short recessions wages and consumer prices have seldom fallen promptly or appreciably, even in the prewar period. The absence of downward pressure on consumer prices has resulted in large part from the unprecedented stability of disposable personal income. The major cause of this has been the "built-in stabilizers"—the automatic fall in tax receipts and rise in transfer payments, especially unemployment insurance benefits, when income falls. Wage increases during recessions may have been a contributing factor in this stability of disposable personal income.

The importance of union influence in creating downward wage rigidity in mild recessions is largely limited to highly competitive industries. In industries dominated by large firms, wage rigidity during recessions and during the early stages of severe depressions antedates the organization of unions. Thus in the period from September, 1929, to September, 1931, there was little or no decrease in money hourly earnings, and there was an increase in real hourly earnings in such industries as automobiles, agricultural implements, electrical manufacturing, iron and steel, meat-packing, and rubber, though all were unorganized and had sharp decreases in hours and employment. It is disagreeable and unpopular to cut wages at any time, and firms are undoubtedly reluctant to do so in the absence of powerful competitive pressures. The principal exception to this generalization in the past forty years occurred in 1920, when the wage level at the start of the depression had been reached during a dizzy inflation and was widely regarded as temporary and abnormal.

Wage increases during recessions are more difficult to explain in the absence of unions. To understand the recent rises in wages when business activity has been declining, we must look more carefully at the wage provisions of long-term union agreements.

§ 7. **Escalator Clauses.** The writing of a new collective agreement in a major bargaining relationship is a long and difficult job. The preparation for negotiations and the negotiations themselves take much time, effort, and expense for both parties. When negotiations break down and there is a major strike, the costs to the parties are of course enormously greater. To avoid the costs and risks of frequent negotiations, parties to collective bargaining have turned increasingly to agreements that run for several years.

For long-term agreements to be acceptable to unions, they must make some provision for the adjustment of wages during the life of the agreement. These provisions have generally been of two sorts. The first is the escalator clause, which provides for periodic changes in money wages if the Consumer Price Index has changed by some specific amount since the beginning of an agreed period. This clause guarantees the union that real wages will not be eroded by inflation during the life of the agreement. The second kind of provision is called the "annual improvement factor" in some agreements; in others it has no special name. It provides for wage increases over and above those resulting from the operation of the escalator clause; that is, for increases in real wages during the life of the agreement. The amount of these increases has sometimes been chosen to bear a rough relation to the average increase in output per man-hour in the economy over some long period. For this reason the provision is often called a productivity clause. In the late 1950's an estimated 3 to 4 million workers were covered by agreements providing for one or both of these types of automatic wage increases.

It has been widely argued that the inclusion of escalator clauses in collective agreements is inflationary. For an escalator clause to operate, there must be a prior change in the Consumer Price Index, so that such clauses could not in themselves initiate an inflation. Perhaps, however, they could accelerate or magnify an inflation that was initiated elsewhere, or conceivably they could even transform a brief random or seasonal price rise into a sustained price rise.

Arguments of this sort are sometimes based on the observations that escalator clauses increase the money incomes of workers and that workers have a high propensity to spend their incomes. However, it must be recognized that wage changes under the terms of escalator clauses are transfers of income among private parties; in this they differ from, say parity prices for farm products, which are paid from the public fisc. The income gained by workers in such a transfer is lost by employers. For the effects of the transfer to be inflationary on the demand side (as distinguished from the cost side), the workers must have a higher propensity to spend than the employers. Note that the propensity in question is not the propensity to consume. Spending on investment goods by employers can be as inflationary as spending on consumer goods. In the short run it may be more so, for there are more likely to be bottlenecks in the capacity to produce investment goods. If we consider the demand side in terms of total spending rather than of consumption, it becomes difficult to support the proposition that transfers of income under escalator clauses increase aggregate demand.

From the cost side wage increases under escalator clauses can raise unit labor costs, lead to new price increases, and thus cause new wage increases under the provisions of the escalator clauses. This is simply a special variant of the general spiral process in which the spiral mechanism is formalized. It is subject to the usual general condition that the increasingly higher levels of wages and prices must be financed if the process is not to break down. To evaluate this aspect of the operation of escalator clauses, we must compare the course of wages under such clauses with their course elsewhere.

Collective bargaining agreements that fixed wages for a period of a year or longer were often disadvantageous to workers when prices rose rapidly. In the years 1946–48 many unions found that their wage gains were quickly cancelled by the rise in consumer prices, and in many cases real wages fell. It was this experience that led to the spread of the escalator clause that began in earnest in 1950. It seems probable that wages and labor costs rise with less lag under inflationary conditions in the presence of escalator clauses than under a system of annual fixed-wage agreements. This is not certain, however, because unions without the protection of an escalator clause will attempt to anticipate future price increases in their annual wage negotiations. This could at times lead to wage increases larger than would be produced by formal escalation, particularly if the union anticipation of continued price increases is exaggerated or incorrect. A comparison of the experience of the steel and automobile industries for the period from mid-1948 to mid-1956 is instructive in this regard. During these years, the automobile workers were covered by escalator clauses, while workers in basic steel were not. Both were organized by similar industrial unions. Average hourly earnings rose at an average annual rate of 6.4 per cent in basic steel and 5.1 per cent in automobiles during this period; moreover, the automobile industry was markedly freer from major strikes.[1]

It is not at all clear that escalator clauses make wages rise faster than they would rise without any collective bargaining. Escalators may merely remove an artificial disadvantage of organized workers during inflations created by earlier forms of collective agreements. Nor is it clear that the kind of annual wage bargaining used in 1946–48 retarded the rise of prices. The saving in labor costs resulting from fixed-wage agreements might have been passed on to consumers in lower prices, but it is doubtful that it actually was. Much of it probably went into windfall profits for small manufacturers and distributors (automobile dealers, for example).

The incomes of some unorganized employees move sluggishly and lag behind price rises in rapid inflations; the salaries of teachers and civil servants are examples. Such salaries are changed only at long intervals, and often by a cumbersome process. It seems doubtful, however, that the wages of manual workers in a free market share this attribute. Most of the evidence that there is a lag of wages behind prices in inflations refers to the distant past; some of it is of poor quality and some applies to periods in which one would expect the real incomes of workers to fall because of increases in the supply of labor or reductions in the real income of the economy. If we can expect wages to respond rather promptly to changes in the price level in non-union markets for manual

[1] See Joseph W. Garbarino, "The Productivity Wage Policy: An Analysis of Escalation" (Washington, D.C.: Brookings Institution, forthcoming), Chapter V.

labor, escalator clauses raise costs only by comparison with other types of bargaining.

One test of whether escalator clauses raise wages faster than they would otherwise have risen is what happens when an agreement containing such a clause expires. Does the employer find that his wages are now too high, and does he insist on reducing them or at least on not increasing them in reaching a new agreement? Or is the union able to make new gains in wages or fringe benefits over and above those obtained during the life of the long-term agreement? In the second case, the escalator clause can reasonably be supposed to govern only the form and timing of the increases that the union could have won under annual bargaining. And the second case has been overwhelmingly the dominant case in the United States since 1948.

In these circumstances the argument that escalator clauses are inflationary must be based on the premise that wage increases under the clauses will be transmitted to the non-union sector and to the unions with annual contracts, so that when the long-term agreement expires wages under it are not out of line on the high side. We have already examined the conditions under which such transmission could be expected, and there is no need to re-examine them here.

It should also be noted that escalator clauses generally provide for downward changes in wages when the Consumer Price Index falls, with some agreed floor below which the clause is no longer operative. Because there have been only very slight declines in the Consumer Price Index, these floors have been of almost no practical significance in the past twelve years. Though the wage decreases under escalator clauses have been few and small, they have created cost reductions that would not have taken place under fixed wage contracts or in the absence of collective bargaining. Because of escalator clauses there may now be somewhat more downward flexibility of wages in mild recessions than there was in the 1920's in such industries as automobiles and steel.

§ 8. The Annual Improvement Factor. The second kind of wage increase under long-term contracts has been the periodic increase in wages over and above the increases resulting from the operation of an escalator clause. This is closely related to a more general expectation that wage increases will be negotiated every year under annual agreements in the absence of special adverse circumstances, and to an even broader expectation on the part of all employees that they will get wage or salary increases from time to time beyond those connected with promotions.

In an economy whose productivity is increasing, most workers can expect to receive increases in real income either through increases in money wages with prices constant (or rising less rapidly than wages) or through falling prices with wages constant. The American economy now seems to be committed to the first of these routes, that of rising money wages. Trade union pressures are an important part of the process that led to this choice. The route chosen has the advantage that it avoids the frictions inherent in reducing prices; it lubricates the process of distributing the income gain. The apparent disadvantage of the wage-increase route for the retired and for other receivers of interest income is probably not a real disadvantage in the long run. Once the route chosen can be predicted, interest rates will be lower for a falling price level than for a stable or gently rising one.

The use of an annual improvement factor or some similar money wage increase to distribute gains in real incomes does not mean that trade unions accept a necessity to limit real wage increases to the rise in productivity in the economy as a whole. Such an acceptance implies the belief that the distribution of income at the beginning of a long-term agreement was an equitable one, and few unions would concede this. For most, it is a continuing article of faith that labor receives too small a share of income and capital too large a share. The actual operation of long-term agreements supports this view. If labor's gains were actually to be limited to those under the escalator and annual improvement clauses, there would never be any need to renegotiate the economic provisions of the agreement, apart from taking account of new evidence on the trend of productivity. In fact, however, when long-term agreements have expired the unions have generally demanded and frequently won new economic concessions, often in the form of additional fringe benefits. This forces us to one of two conclusions: either the wage increases under the long-term agreements were too small to reflect the full gains in productivity in the economy, or the unions have made real gains that in total exceed the rate of productivity increase. From more general evidence on the relation between real wages and productivity, the latter seems far more probable.

If acceptance of the proposition that wages should not rise more than output per man-hour in the economy as a whole is not implied by the existence of annual improvement factors, the proposition is nevertheless widely accepted outside the labor movement. It has been stated by employers, by academic economists, and by President Eisenhower in his economic reports. Usually the statement is made that money wage increases in excess of productivity increases are inflationary. This implies that to prevent inflation we must prevent any increase in the wage-earner's share of income, or that no such increase is possible. There is indeed no particular reason why employers, economists, or government officials should regard the wage-earner's share of income as too small at the present time, but this is not to say that it ought to be frozen at its present level. Economic forces have produced changes in the wage-earner's share in the past, and they will undoubtedly produce further changes in the future. It is not possible to predict whether these changes will work to raise or to lower the wage-earner's share. Freezing the share, however, like the freezing of any price or income in a changing economy, will sooner or later have unfortunate consequences for resource allocation. It is probably to the good that efforts in this direction have been confined to exhortation, which is seldom a potent economic force.

On this view there is no general reason to deplore the fact

that unions with escalator clauses and annual improvement factors can make additional gains when their long-term agreements expire. In particular cases, these gains may not have been appropriate to the circumstances of the industries or companies that granted them, but that is another matter. The opposite proposition also follows—at times the wage increases called for by long-term agreements may be too large rather than too small. It might then be in the general interest for unions to forego increases to which they are entitled under prior agreements—for example, if a wage increase during a recession through its effect on costs would tend to delay recovery. At other times, a moratorium on wage increases after the expiration of a contract might be desirable.

In general, however, union spokesmen reject the position that wage increases during recession tend to delay the recovery. Unions view the effects of wage changes largely from the side of purchasing power. They argue that recessions are caused by inadequate purchasing power, and that therefore wage increases during prosperity will help to prevent recessions and wage increases during recessions will help to end them.

It is of course a mistake to ignore the effects of wage changes on demand, as many economists once did in arguing that recessions can be cured by wage cuts. But it is equally a mistake to ignore the effects on costs as the unions do. Cost and price increases during a recession are likely to lead to reductions in output at least as large as any increases in output stimulated by the increased purchases of wage-earners. The probable predominance of cost effects over income effects in these circumstances arises in part because much spending in a recession is not from wage income. Some is from liquid savings and some from transfer payments, especially unemployment insurance benefits, whose amount is not immediately affected by a rise in wages. Price rises will reduce the volume of production represented by this spending and the employment furnished in producing it.

However, many special arguments can be developed about

the predominance of cost effects or purchasing-power effects under particular circumstances. Perhaps none have enough generality to be safe guides to wage policy for the whole economy. In the present state of economic knowledge, it seems wisest to avoid deliberate manipulation of wages in countercyclical policy, and to rely on measures that act in an unambiguous direction. This is true of a wide range of monetary and fiscal measures. On this reasoning, the operation of annual improvement factors during recessions can be considered mildly mischievous—somewhat more likely than not to be harmful to the economy.

CHAPTER VI

ENTRY TO UNIONS AND UNION SECURITY

§ **1. Union Control of Job Opportunities.** In an economy that
has experienced depressions marked by mass unemployment,
manual workers look upon a steady job as a right to guard
jealously. The leading theory of the American labor movement, that of Selig Perlman, uses this sense of limited job
opportunities to explain the rise of business unionism or
"job-conscious unionism" and many of its important characteristics.[1] The central role of the union is seen as establishing
control over jobs and safeguarding them for its members.
As parts of this function, the union regulates entry into the
trade and into its own membership, establishes jurisdictional
boundaries and patrols them against the incursions of other
unions, creates seniority rights in jobs, and seeks to maintain
or increase the number of jobs in the trade. Some of these
functions will be discussed in this chapter and some in the
following two. The measures the union takes to secure its
own existence as an organization are closely related to its
control over entry and membership and will be discussed in
connection with it.

Those who approach the union from the standpoint of
economic theory, rather than from an institutional and
historical position as Perlman did, would also expect control
of entry to be a crucial union function. They emphasize,

[1] Selig Perlman, *A Theory of the Labor Movement* (New York:
Macmillan, 1928).

121

however, that the scarcity of job opportunities in the union sector does not result entirely from depressions and other forces external to the union. By raising the relative wages of its members, an effective union decreases the number of jobs available for them and at the same time it makes the trade more attractive to those not already in it. It thus tends to create an excess supply of labor in the trade even in periods of prosperity.

The excess supply of labor can appear at three different points, which correspond to three strategies open to the union. It can appear as a pool of applicants for scarce places in a training program, as a pool of qualified workers seeking admission to the union, or as a pool of workers acceptable to the union seeking jobs from employers. The corresponding strategies may be called the apprenticeship strategy, the closed-shop strategy, and the union-shop strategy.

§ 2. **Apprenticeship.** Apprenticeship is the moden survival of a formal system of on-the-job training for the crafts whose traditions date back to the medieval guilds. What is meant here by the apprenticeship strategy is the use of limitation of the number of people trained to raise the earnings of the qualified workers or journeymen.

If a union could effectively limit the total number of people who learned a craft, there would never be more than a temporary oversupply of journeymen. The sense of limited job opportunity would disappear, to be replaced at a different level by a sense of limited training opportunity. The union would seldom have occasion to deny membership to a fully qualified worker. It would not need to strike or bargain over wages, since the restriction of the supply of trained labor would in itself insure that wages would be bid up by the competition of employers.

None of the organizations ordinarily regarded as unions relies primarily on the apprenticeship strategy. Limiting access to training is, however, the basic strategy of a leading union-like organization, the American Medical Association, and seems to have made possible a high return to the skills of physicians without bargaining or strikes. The closest approach to this strategy among the true unions is the combination of apprenticeship and licensing in such crafts as barbers, plumbers, and electricians.[1] The supply of licensed journeymen can be limited and controlled by the union in cities or states where the union uses influence or position on the licensing body to restrict licenses to those who have served a union apprenticeship. There will then be an excess supply of journeymen trained elsewhere, often in small towns, who would like to enter the locality and cannot be licensed. (This case has an analogy in medicine in the treatment of doctors trained in other countries.)

Since union apprenticeship programs do not account for the majority of people who learn any of the unionized crafts, one may wonder why unions participate in apprenticeship programs for unlicensed occupations. Several answers are possible. First, the members of craft unions take pride in their skills. They are proud of their ability to provide employers with highly competent workmen, and they want their sons and nephews entering the trade to receive good training. Second, the work of apprentices near the end of their training may be a good substitute for the work of journeymen. The union seeks to control apprentices to discourage employers from using them for what it considers to be journeyman's work. Unions therefore set wages for apprentices and limit the number trained in union shops even if this does not limit the total supply of journeymen. If the wages of apprentices are set high and the task of training them is burdensome, employers may not want to use as many as the union permits and the limitation on numbers will be superfluous. The limitation on numbers will also be superfluous if the wage is set so low or the term of apprenticeship is so long as to discourage entry into the apprenticeship program.

[1] See Simon Rottenberg, "The Economics of Occupational Licensing," paper presented at a conference on labor economics, Princeton, N.J., April, 1960 (National Bureau of Economic Research, forthcoming).

§3. The Closed Shop.   Since unions do not fully control the channels of training for their trades, they must rely primarily on the power to strike and on collective bargaining to raise relative wages.   They thus tend to create an excess supply of qualified workers.   A union uses the closed shop if it wants to determine which of these workers are employed and the union shop if it does not.   In a closed shop, only those who are already members of the union can be hired by the employer. A union shop permits the employer to select according to his own criteria, provided that the new employees join the union within a stipulated period—usually thirty days.   (Because the closed shop is illegal under the Taft-Hartley Act, agreements that are in practice closed-shop agreements are usually written as union-shop agreements.)

The basic purposes of the closed shop and the union shop are in part different.   The closed shop rations scarce jobs among applicants and also assists in maintaining the union as an organization.   The union shop performs only the second function, except as it excludes the very few job applicants who are unwilling to join a union.   The second function gives to provisions of this general type the generic name of "union security clauses."

A comparison between the apprenticeship strategy and the closed-shop strategy should make clear why the closed shop is regarded here as primarily a rationing device rather than a device to restrict the supply of labor.   A union can restrict the supply of labor by controlling training, or it can raise wages by bargaining, but it cannot ordinarily do both at once.   One or the other must usually be largely superfluous.   If the wage resulting from the restriction on entry is higher than the bargained wage, workers will receive more than the union rate and the bargaining will at best perform a mopping-up function. On the other hand, if the bargained wage is higher than that implied by the limitation of numbers, there will still be an excess of journeymen at the union rate.   Control of entry to the union will then determine which of these can get work but will not directly raise wages.   The two devices can be used effectively together where the demand for labor fluctuates too rapidly to be reflected in changes in the number trained. Bargaining then sets the wage when demand is weak, and limitations of numbers raises the wage when demand is strong. This analysis helps us account for the fact that skilled building trades workers are at times paid more than the union rate.

The closed-shop unions also have a second way of dealing with fluctuating demand. They often keep the number of members low enough so that members get steady work except in seasons when there is no work in the trade. Temporary peaks in demand are then met by issuing work permits to non-members (sometimes at a fee exceeding the dues of members). These permits are subject to cancellation or are good only for short periods. The union could refuse to issue permits and could use the temporary shortage of labor to drive up pay in the peak seasons. However, the full exploitation of such temporary shortages might result in rates so high as to provoke a hostile public reaction.

The argument of the preceding paragraphs is not changed if the union requires the employer to use more men on a job than he would choose to; that is, if it forces him off his demand curve for labor to the right by offering him an all-or-none bargain. Employers will still have a demand at the union rate for a certain number of crews of the required size, and if these do not employ the whole membership, the closed shop will still ration the available positions. If there is a shortage of labor under the requirement, then the requirement together with the limited number of available workers tends to establish a wage above the union rate, and there is little need for wage bargaining.

Unions that operate under closed-shop arrangements ordinarily have hiring halls that refer unemployed members to employers reporting vacancies. When the Taft-Hartley Act made the closed shop illegal in interstate commerce, some of these hiring halls began to make token referrals of non-members but were seldom effectively opened to them. In 1958 the National Labor Relations Board began to impose severe penalties on unions whose hiring halls did not operate according to rules designed to protect the rights of non-members. However, a Supreme Court decision early in 1961 held that the NLRB had exceeded its authority under the law in its policy on hiring halls. The board still appears to be free to act where specific cases of discrimination against non-members can be proved.

Other union devices for reserving work for members are also presumably still legal. Some unions have established separate lists for referrals, one carrying the names of those who have worked in the trade in their locality before, the other for newcomers. Referrals are made from the second list only when the first is exhausted. Where a closed shop has been in effect, the first list would contain only members at the outset, and others would get on it only very slowly.

The closed shop has value for a union only if it wants to fill available openings in a way different from the one employers would use to fill them if left to their own devices. For example, the union may want to give preference to sons of members, while the employers might feel that these were not always the best-qualified applicants. In other cases, however, the employer may have so many applicants, all of whom seem well qualified, that he would give preference to the sons of present employees as a way of maintaining good will. If union and employer preferences coincide in this way, the union loses nothing in giving up the closed shop and the employer nothing in granting it.

It is sometimes suggested that a closed shop is itself not objectionable, but a closed union is, and that the law should permit the combination of the closed shop and the open union. If the closed shop is primarily a rationing device, this combination destroys its basic purpose. It would be of interest to unions only as a substitute for the union shop in industries like construction where the short duration of the individual job may make the union shop difficult to administer.

§ **4. Entry to the Union.**[1]   Under an effective closed shop, the union rations employment opportunities by its selection of members and the operation of its hiring hall.   Two basic types of rationing are open to it—price rationing and non-price rationing.   In price rationing the initiation fees would be set high enough to keep the number of applicants equal to the number of openings and no further selection of members would be needed.   The present members would in effect collect from new entrants a sum equal to the capitalized value of the differential in earnings created by the union over the expected working life of the new member.[2]

Reports filed by unions under the reporting and disclosure provisions of the Landrum-Griffin Act have recently given us for the first time a comprehensive picture of the initiation fees, dues, and work permit fees of local unions.   Monthly dues are most frequently in the range of $3.00 to $5.00; this range included about half of the 40,000 unions reporting.   The most frequent initiation fee was $5.00.   However, of approximately 39,000 local unions reporting, 325 had initiation fees from $250.01 to $500.00 and 17 had initiation fees from $500.01 to $1,400.00.   Of approximately 48,000 locals giving information on work permits, about 6,000 issued such permits for a fee.   The most frequent range of fees was $3.00 to

[1] For a more complete discussion of this topic along similar lines, see Gary S. Becker, "Union Restrictions on Entry" in Philip D. Bradley (ed.), *The Public Stake in Union Power* (Charlottesville: University of Virginia Press, 1959).

[2] It might seem that high monthly dues as well as high initiation fees can be used for price rationing.   However, dues are paid by all members, old as well as new.   They will ordinarily be matched by some sort of benefits accruing to all members.   Thus an increase in dues will ordinarily either increase the perquisites of membership or will be used to win a still further increase in wages, and thus will fail to perform a rationing function.   High dues will serve as a rationing device only when dues are equal for all members, but benefits are greater for old members.   Cases of this sort may exist where wages or earnings rise sharply with seniority, so that the union makes much larger gains for its senior members than for its junior ones, and where the number of jobs at the top is not growing.

$3.99 per month, but 104 locals reported monthly fees from $50.00 to $147.75.[1]

This evidence does not suggest that any union with sub-stantial impact on relative wages charges initiation fees or dues high enough to ration openings by these devices alone. Some idea of the amounts that would be involved in such rationing can be obtained by looking at the sums paid for transfer of the rights to operate a taxicab or a tavern in cities where licenses to engage in these pursuits are limited in number and transferable. Becker reports that New York City taxicab medallions have sold for about $17,000 in recent years, and San Francisco papers in 1959 reported a figure of $16,000 for the transfer of licenses to operate a taxicab in that city. The value of entry to a union with a 20 per cent effect on relative earnings would be of this order of magnitude even at fairly high interest rates.[2]

There are at least two reasons why unions do not rely on open price rationing to select members. First, initiation fees of the required size would shock the public, and, in most cases, the members of the union. Second, the high initiation fee would be an advertisement of the union's monopoly power and might lead to public efforts at limiting this power or to increase employer resistance. There may still be instances of corrupt price rationing—unions whose officers or business agents collect high payments from new entrants for their personal use. For the most part, however, the closed-shop unions have used non-price rationing. This takes the form of discrimination against groups not wanted in the union and favoritism toward preferred groups.

The principal identifiable discrimination has been against Negroes. At one time several national craft unions had constitutional provisions restricting membership to whites.

[1] *Monthly Labor Review*, January, 1961, based on the first annual report of the Bureau of Labor-Management Reports.

[2] Membership in a union with an effect of 20 per cent on annual earnings would increase earnings $1,000 a year for a man whose alternative earnings were $5,000. The present value of an annuity of $1,000 a year for 40 years is over $15,000 at an interest rate of 6 per cent.

The written color bar has now all but disappeared, in part because of pressures from the AFL–CIO, which favors equal opportunities for all races. However, there are still many all-white local unions. In some cases this results from discrimination by employers rather than by the union; in others it results from an unwritten union rule. As sentiment in the labor movement and in American society at large moves more strongly against racial discrimination of all forms, discrimination of this type will undoubtedly be diminished in admission to closed-shop unions.

Preference for the sons and nephews of members is the most conspicuous form of favoritism in trade unions as it is in medicine. In other cases unions may favor friends of members or workers whose national origin is the same as that of a large group within the membership.

§ 5. The Union Shop.   The union shop is now by far the most common form of union security provision in collective bargaining agreements. An analysis of 1631 major agreements covering about 7.5 million workers in 1958–59 showed that 74 per cent of these workers were covered by union-shop provisions. These presumably include some that were in effect closed shops. About one-fourth of the workers covered by union-shop provisions were in modified union shops that excepted certain groups of workers (for example, those already employed when the first union-shop agreement was reached). Maintenance of membership, which will be discussed below, covered 7 per cent of the total number of workers. The remaining 19 per cent were covered by agreements having no union security provision except that they gave the union sole bargaining rights.[1]

In general, industrial unions have not wanted to participate in the hiring process. This reluctance arises in part because they bargain for a great variety of crafts and occupations and would find it difficult to operate a hiring hall as craft unions do. Because the membership of these unions was usually

[1] *Monthly Labor Review*, December, 1959.

heterogeneous when they were organized and because political radicals were prominent in the organization of many of them, they have never had a tradition of racial discrimination as national organizations, though some pockets of discrimination have survived in the South and in skilled labor categories. Moreover, control of entrants is less important to unions whose members do not shift frequently from one employer to another. For these unions seniority and promotion from within protect the old member against competition from the new entrant.

When industrial unions were first organized in the mass-production industries, most workers were eager to join. A few, however, did not join voluntarily. Among these was a very small number of workers who would not join because of principle or religious belief; a larger number were reluctant to pay union dues and felt that they would enjoy the benefits of collective bargaining whether they joined or not.

The workers in this last group are called "free riders" by union members. The unions reason that since all workers in the bargaining unit receive the benefits of bargaining, and since the union is obligated by law to process the grievances of non-members, all workers in the unit should pay their share of the costs. Collective bargaining is viewed as a form of industrial government in which dues correspond to the taxes paid by all citizens, whether they choose to participate or not. This argument has both a good deal of appeal and an important flaw. Union activities are not confined to collective bargaining; they include among other things political activity. Although unions cannot make cash contributions out of dues to candidates for federal office, they can work in their behalf and they can make cash contributions from dues at the state and local level in many states. The member may thus find his dues used to support candidates to whom he is bitterly opposed, and this may be a factor in some decisions not to join a union.[1]

[1] One method of solving this problem is "contracting out," a system long used in Britain. Under one form of this system, unions can make political contributions from dues, but any member can direct that his

In the absence of a union shop, unions use informal methods of dealing with the free rider.   The simplest and most effective force is simply the disapproval of his fellow workers.   In stubborn cases he may be sent to Coventry or may have a series of close escapes from serious accidents.   Some unions have set up dues picket lines, which on certain days patrolled the plant gates and refused admission to non-members, costing them a day's pay.   As unions mature, they feel that new workers are more and more likely to take the union for granted.   The young worker often has had no experience with non-union conditions.   The free-rider problem is expected to grow, and the unions increasingly have sought the union shop to deal with it.

It has been argued that the union shop is unfair because some unions do not raise the wages of their members, and in those that do, not all members benefit.   Other union activities, such as grievance settlement, frequently involve the adjudication of disputes in which the interests of various members conflict; in seniority disputes this must always be the case. The argument is that workers who feel that they do not individually benefit from the union should be free to stay out.[1] The argument does not meet the union position that collective bargaining is a form of industrial government.   One cannot argue that citizens should not be taxed to support a system of

portion of the contributions be given instead to some charity of his choice. It could also be provided that his share be given to some other political cause of his choice.   The union's political decisions as an organization remain important, because only members with strong opposite convictions will take the trouble to contract out.   Refunding money to the worker would be unacceptable to American unions because it would create an incentive to express disagreement even where the worker had no opinions on the campaign.

In June, 1961, the United States Supreme Court decided that the use of dues funds of unwilling members for political purposes by a railway union was not permitted by the union-shop provision of the Railway Labor Act. The decision appears to invite aggrieved members to sue for refunds of dues.

[1] See Philip D. Bradley, *Involuntary Participation in Unionism* (Washington, D.C.: American Enterprise Association, 1956).

civil courts merely because any damages awarded the plaintiffs must be paid by the defendants. All citizens benefit from having an orderly way of settling their claims against one another.

In general, the union shop has faced bitter employer opposition, and in many industries it has been won only after long strikes. Employers see the union as analagous to a private club or social organization, not to a government. They argue that no one should be coerced to join a private organization by economic pressure, or should lose his job because he is expelled from such an organization or is denied admission to it.

There has also been some opposition to the union shop among radical minorities within the union movement. They have argued that the unwilling member is not an asset to the union, and that the union will be stronger if every member has been persuaded to join. With the general decline of union radicalism, this position is less often met. The union shop is a great convenience in union administration and increases the financial resources of the union. Most unionists equate opposition to the union shop with a desire to weaken unions. They also argue that the union shop makes unions more responsible, since in its absence the leaders may feel it necessary to press weak grievances or to make extravagant demands in an effort to win or hold members.

Two less exacting types of union security clause are sometimes used where a union is unable to win a union shop. One is the "agency shop" in which workers are not required to join the union, but are required to make payments in lieu of dues if they do not. In the statistics cited at the beginning of this section, agency shops have been included with modified union shops. A still weaker provision is the "maintenance of membership" clause, which provides that a worker who joins the union must remain a member in good standing for the duration of the collective bargaining agreement. This clause was originally introduced by the War Labor Board in World War II as a compromise between the union demand for a union shop and management opposition to all union security clauses. It does not require anyone to join a union or make payments to it in the first instance. As the union shop has spread, the maintenance of membership clause has frequently been displaced.

Financial security is also provided to the union by the check-off, a widely used device. The check-off means that the employer deducts union dues from the paychecks of the members and transmits them to the union in a lump sum.

§ 6. **Legal Restrictions on the Union Shop.** The opposition of employers and some other groups, such as farm organizations, to the union shop and the closed shop has been reflected in a series of legislative restrictions on union security provisions. In 1947 the Taft-Hartley Act outlawed the closed shop in employment affecting interstate commerce, though the restriction has been largely ineffective in practice. The Taft-Hartley Act also imposed a number of restrictions on the union shop. First, it provided that a union shop could be negotiated only where it had received the prior approval of a majority of the workers in the bargaining unit in an election conducted by the National Labor Relations Board. The union shop was approved in such an overwhelming majority of all such elections and received so large a majority of the votes cast that this provision was soon repealed.[1]

The second restriction on the union shop provided that the union could not require the discharge of any worker under the

[1] The provision is an example of a fallacy about worker loyalties and decisions that has persisted in employer and legislative thinking despite the mass of evidence against it. The fallacy consists in assuming that an issue that is controversial in the body politic as a whole will also be controversial among workers or among union members, and that they will consider it on its merits as an isolated issue if they are permitted to vote in a free election. In fact, workers perceive the issue as whether they are for or against their union. Where the election is conducted in a unionized plant, an overwhelming vote for the union position is a foregone conclusion. The same fallacy is involved in the provision of the Taft-Hartley Act that calls for a vote on the employer's last offer in an emergency dispute.

terms of a union-shop agreement except for failure to tender the dues and initiation fees applicable to all members.   This provision protects the jobs of political dissidents who may be expelled from the union.   The protection is less than complete in two respects.   First, the expelled member, though he retains his job, loses his right to participate in decisions about his conditions of work.   Second, there is nothing to prevent the employer from discharging expelled members for some alleged cause even if the union does not request it, and the union can hardly be expected to defend him vigorously under the circumstances.   An employer may discharge the expelled worker because he feels it will promote good relations with the union or will reduce tensions in the shop, or because he shares the union feeling against the man involved (as for example, in cases of expulsion for Communist activity).

Under these circumstances, the worker's main recourse is to file a complaint with the National Labor Relations Board charging the union, the employer, or both with an unfair labor practice.   In recent years, complaints filed by individuals have been a majority of all unfair labor practice complaints filed with the board, though of course most of these are not of this particular kind.

3   The last provision of the Taft-Hartley Act relating to the union shop is the one that has made the state "right to work" laws so important.   It provides that where a state prohibits the union shop, this prohibition shall have force even in establishments covered by the federal labor relations laws. A provision giving precedence to state over federal law in an area subject to federal jurisdiction is highly unusual and it has been bitterly opposed by the unions.

Important   The state "right to work" laws provide that no one shall be required to belong to a union or not to belong to a union as a condition of employment, and that no collective agreement shall impose such a requirement.   The prohibition against requiring workers not to belong to a union outlaws the yellow-dog contract, which has been unenforceable in federal jurisdiction since 1932 and illegal since 1935.   Since the yellow-dog

contract has not been of recent importance, the real effect of
the "right to work" laws has been to outlaw the union shop.
The name is a misnomer, since it suggests that the laws make
some kind of general guarantee of full employment. Such
laws are now in effect in eighteen states, including one important
industrial state (Indiana). The best available study of the
operation of these laws suggests strongly that they have had
little actual effect.[1]   Bootleg closed shops have been common
under these laws as they have under federal laws. The unions
that use the union shop have reverted to their informal
methods of dealing with or living with non-members and do
not seem to have lost much bargaining strength. Nevertheless, the "right to work" laws have been a source of prolonged
and acrimonious controversy in many states. They have been
a potent symbol of the differences in political and social
philosophy between unions on the one hand and employers,
farmers, and small-town businessmen on the other. Employers and unions alike seem to feel, without any very
convincing evidence, that these laws are a real blow to union
power.[2]   A few unusually consistent political conservatives
have opposed the "right to work" laws on the ground that
they restrict the freedom of contract between employers and
unions.

[1] Frederic Meyers, "*Right to Work*" *in Practice* (New York: Fund for
the Republic, 1959).

[2] Union literature frequently stresses the fact that wages are lower in
states that have these laws. This is a classic example of a false inference
from a true fact, since these were low-wage states before there were any
such laws. The same social and economic characteristics of these states
that made them low-wage states to begin with enabled the laws to pass.

CHAPTER VII

UNION PRACTICES AFFECTING EMPLOYMENT AND PRODUCTIVITY

§ 1. Working Rules That Increase the Number Employed. The discussion thus far has assumed that wages are set in collective bargaining and that the employer is left free to hire the amount of labor he wants at these wages. Although this is usually the case, it is not always. The union need not take the number of jobs at each rate as given; it can force the employer to use more men at each rate than he would choose to. Some unions specify the number of men to be used for particular tasks; others require unnecessary work to be done, or require the use of inefficient methods.

The effect of unions on efficiency is a controversial area in industrial relations, as can be seen from the terms used in discussing it. In objecting to a rapid pace of work, unions talk of speed-ups and sweatshops; employers discuss union working rules in terms of feather-bedding. Issues of efficiency become entangled with those of health and safety, and the effect of the union as an organization is often hard to distinguish from the informal restriction of output practiced by work groups.

The simplest kind of union rule affecting the number employed is a full crew rule, a rule specifying the minimum number of men to be employed for a given task. Such rules are of great importance in the railroad industry, where the full crew requirements were written into state law in seventeen

136

states as of 1959. The railroads feel that these laws require them to use many extra men; the unions claim that these men perform a necessary function.

A leading issue in this area concerns the need for a fireman on diesel locomotives in freight and yard service. In 1958 a Canadian Royal Commission reached a unanimous decision that firemen were not needed in such operations. At the present time (June, 1961) a Presidential Board is investigating this and related issues affecting railroads in the United States.

The musicians' union also has a kind of full crew rule by which it specifies the minimum size of bands that can perform on various occasions. It sometimes requires as well that standby bands of local musicians be hired, even if they do not play, while visiting "name bands" are performing.

Rules of the same general kind can require extra work rather than extra people. For example, the typographers' union requires that advertising material received by a newspaper as mats (papier mâché matrices from which preset type is cast) be reset at a later date. The mat is used to save time; the reset material, or bogus, is scrapped and serves only to give work to local compositors. The cost of the rule to the employer is reduced if the bogus can be set in slack periods when there is not enough other work to occupy the full number of compositors employed.

Makework requirements have at times been imposed by several of the building trades unions. For example, many painters' locals long prohibited the use of spray guns. The importance of such practices in the building trades seems to have diminished in recent years, perhaps as a result of the high level of employment experienced since World War II.

Union rules that increase the number of workers on a job do not necessarily increase employment in the trade. The restrictive rules either add to the price of the product, which will reduce the amount bought, or they will induce employers to contract their scale of operations. These effects could sometimes offset or exceed the original gain in employment. Such a result would, of course, represent a miscalculation by the union and a union that was aware of it would presumably rescind the make-work rule.

Unions have a limited ability to strike and to impose losses on employers, and must decide how much of this power to use in raising wages and how much to use in increasing employment at a given wage through restrictive work rules. In this sense, the restrictive rule is an alternative to a still higher wage for a smaller number of members, which could have been won by using the union's full power in the wage dimension. Nevertheless, a strong union may be able to achieve a position at least temporarily, in which both employment and wages are higher than they would be in the absence of a union.[1]

The rules discussed in this section are characteristic of craft unions. Where industrial unions participate in the restriction of output, it is usually by the less formal devices discussed in § 3.

§ 2. Negotiating Changes in Working Rules. When a restrictive working rule has been in effect for a long time, it becomes extremely difficult to negotiate its abandonment. There is likely to be a sharp divergence in attitude toward such rules between the union and management. Management, along with the middle class in general and economists in particular, regards efficiency and hard work as virtues. This attitude has strong moral and ethical overtones that go well beyond its simple economic meaning; the restriction of output is viewed as not merely wasteful but sinful. The unskilled or semi-skilled manual worker does not share these attitudes. Because his work is often arduous or monotonous, he regards it as perfectly legitimate to dislike it, and will cheer loudly if the assembly line breaks down. He may regard the management attitude as insincere or as based on a double standard, in part because he does not consider some of management's duties to

---

[1] For a formal analysis of this possibility, see G. Warren Nutter, "The Limits of Union Power," in Philip D. Bradley (ed.), *The Public Stake in Union Power* (Charlottesville: University of Virginia Press, 1959), pp. 291–94.

be real work. Whereas management publications deplore the length of workers' coffee breaks, union publications stress the size of executive expense accounts.

Apart from this general difference in attitudes, unions and work groups develop a specific rationale for particular restrictive practices, since no one likes to think of himself as useless or parasitic. Thus the fireman on the diesel engine suggests the possibility that the engineer may drop dead, and the occurrence of one such incident will reinforce his defense for years. If trains are equipped with a device that brings them to a stop if something happens to the engineer, the fireman will point out that the device may fail.

Underlying all such arguments is the fact that eliminating restrictive practices means displacing some people from their jobs. The workers and their unions regard the right to a job as a property right, not to be infringed without compensation. If a diesel fireman is no longer needed, this is no fault of the man who began his career in good faith as a coal-shovelling fireman on a steam locomotive, and he sees no reason why he should suffer from the change. Although his conception may have no legal foundation, management in practice may be forced to accept it and to make concessions in other ways in order to get the restrictive rules changed. It is sometimes provided that present incumbents of jobs will not be affected by the change; thus the Canadian railroads no longer need to hire new firemen for freight and yard service but have agreed not to discharge their present ones. Wage increases and dismissal compensation can sometimes be used to win agreement on rules changes. Since the corporation with its perpetual life and its good access to capital markets is likely to have a longer time horizon than the worker, there will usually be some terms on which both parties feel the new situation to be better than the old.

In the absence of voluntary agreement between unions and management to eliminate working rules that reduce output, it may sometimes be appropriate for the government to require the abolition of the rules (perhaps through binding arbitration) and set the compensation if any to be paid to the workers adversely affected. Such an action would, of course, only be appropriate if the working rule is found not to have a material bearing on the health and safety of workers or consumers.[1]

§ 3. Restriction of Output. Work groups often develop standards for a maximum fair day's work and apply effective informal sanctions to those who produce more.[2] Such practices have at least three purposes. First, they can be attempts to prolong the life of a job; if a work group expects to be laid off when seasonal orders are filled, they will stretch out their last work as long as possible. Second, the limitation of output can be used to prevent a work pace that is too rapid for the least able workers. Output may be limited for this reason even if it is technically possible for each worker to work at his own pace; the purpose in these circumstances is to prevent the discipline or discharge of the less able worker. Finally, restriction of output is frequently used as a way of getting the most out of piece rate or incentive wage systems. If workers discover a way of making very high earnings on a particular operation, they often restrict output to hold earnings to a figure that management regards as reasonable, and this prevents the cutting of the rate. If an incentive rate is set at which earnings are usually low, workers may restrict output sharply and earn only their minimum guarantee. Unit costs will be very high in such cases, and management may be forced to set a more liberal rate in order to reduce them. Thus the operation of the incentive system can become a game in which the worker and management are continuously seeking to best one another. Often management

[1] The concept of property rights in jobs can be traced back to the writings of John R. Commons and Selig Perlman. I am indebted to Professor William Gomberg for calling my attention to its importance in this context.

[2] See Stanley B. Mathewson, *Restriction of Output among Unorganized Workers* (New York: Viking Press, 1931). See also Donald Roy "Quota Restriction and Goldbricking in a Machine Shop," *American Journal of Sociology*, March 1952.

sets up a system that assumes that workers respond only to direct monetary incentives, and then criticizes the "selfish" worker who adapts his response to this kind of atmosphere.

Restriction of output is found both in union and non-union plants. In union plants, restrictive devices may be used without any participation by the union as an organization, or the union may be involved in some way. The union is most likely to be involved in setting the pace of work in an operation under time rates. For example, if workers feel that the speed of an assembly line is too fast, they can file a formal grievance and the union will be involved in settling it. It is typical for collective agreements to provide that piece rates or incentive rates will not be reset during the life of the agreement unless there is a change in the nature of the operation or unless the union consents. Conflict often arises over whether changes in an operation are sufficient basis for a change in the rate, and the union may suspect management of initiating changes in an operation solely to get a "loose" rate reduced.

Where there is strong protection against the lowering of rates that yield high earnings, this may tend to prevent restriction of output whose purpose is to disguise "loose" incentive rates. Since few incentive plans give workers the whole saving in unit cost resulting from high rates of output, unit costs can be lower with such protection than under informal restriction of output.

The widespread existence of restriction of output under non-union conditions does not mean that restrictive union rules never add to costs or that they merely codify the practices that would be followed in any case. There is an important distinction between informal restriction of output and the kind of make-work rule discussed in the preceding section. Restriction of output under non-union conditions depends essentially on concealing the restriction from management. As each ruse or trick is discovered, the workers must develop new ones. They may always succeed in doing so and may always hold output considerably below that which could be achieved if each worked at a pace that required his full energy.

Nevertheless, new techniques can always be introduced, and the trend of productivity through time need not be affected. In contrast, the formal restrictive rules of the craft unions can prevent the introduction of new techniques or nullify their effect in lowering labor requirements. Only a strong trade union could require a railroad to employ a fireman on a diesel freight engine if the railroad did not believe that his work was necessary.

§ 4. **Union-Management Co-operation.** While some unions have attempted to limit productivity and to restrict output, others have actively participated in plans to increase productivity. Union efforts of this sort are usually called "union-management co-operation." The most frequent origin of such plans is a competitive threat to the survival of a firm or a plant. If the union becomes convinced that the jobs of its members can be saved only by increasing their productivity, the development of a co-operative plan to cut costs is often possible. In other cases, the plan may be inspired by a desire to increase earnings. Of course, such plans are unlikely to develop where bargaining relations have been hostile or marked by great suspicion. They are also unlikely to develop in the largest and most profitable firms, where the union will be more concerned with getting a larger share of existing revenues. For example, it is difficult to imagine the development of a formal plan of union-management co-operation to improve productivity between the United Auto Workers and General Motors. The union will also be more concerned about saving jobs where alternative jobs are scarce and poor than where they are plentiful and good. For this reason, unions may more frequently be concerned with productivity in small towns than in big cities.

The success of union-management co-operation is possible because almost all work groups find ways of improving the efficiency of the operations they know so well, and many of these ways are not obvious to managers or engineers. The accumulation of many small improvements in techniques can have a large aggregate effect. Management often tries to harness this source of progress through suggestion systems, but for a variety of reasons, such systems seldom achieve their full potential. Often the rewards are too small to be effective, or the workers do not have confidence that they will get credit for their suggestions. Workers may fear that their suggestions will lead to a reduction in employment or will prefer to save them as private ways of easing the job and coping with peak work loads.

Under a successful plan of union-management co-operation, the potential for improvement is released by reducing the worker's suspicions of management and by creating large incentives for increased productivity. Perhaps the best known plan at the present time is the Scanlon plan, which involves the use of plant-wide earnings incentives based on cost reductions. It increases the extent of group participation in proposing innovations; it brings in indirect workers, such as maintenance men, often left out of individual incentive plans; and it reduces the tendency for the private hoarding of innovations.

In addition to releasing the potential for innovations, a plan of union-management co-operation can also lead to the relaxation of informal group restrictions on output under existing techniques. The unusually able worker who was held back by the ostracism of "rate-busters" is freed to work up to his capacity when his fellow workers feel that they are benefited rather than "shown up" by his exertions.

§ 5. Protecting and Expanding the Union's Jurisdiction.

This section is not concerned with union efforts to organize unorganized workers but rather with attempts to broaden the definition of the work that is reserved for its present members and with attempts to prevent others from doing this work. Like make-work rules, broadening the jurisdiction is an attempt to create more jobs for the members of the union.

One set of rules protecting the work reserved for the members prohibits apprentices, foremen, helpers, or employers from doing the work of journeymen. These rules are particularly important in contract construction, where the small contractor is frequently a former skilled worker. He is not permitted to mix his entrepreneurial function with work at his old trade if his workers are union members.

Bitter jurisdictional disputes often arise when two craft unions claim the same work for their members. If the employer awards the work to one union, the members of the other will strike, and the employer is caught in the middle. Such disputes are most likely to occur when a change in techniques or materials creates new jobs not exactly like the previous jobs of any craft. Because the Taft-Hartley Act made jurisdictional strikes unfair labor practices for unions, the building trades unions have set up a rather effective system for the arbitration of jurisdictional disputes.

As production worker employment in manufacturing has declined in recent years, industrial unions have increasingly become involved in protecting work for their members. This has led to disputes over "contracting out," which occur when the employer transfers to an outside contractor work that has traditionally been done by members of the bargaining unit. Examples of work that has caused disputes of this type are minor construction, the installation of new machinery, the operation of a plant cafeteria, or washing windows. Some unions have obtained specific clauses in their agreements governing contracting out; others may claim that contracting out violates the union-recognition clause.[1] When disputes over contracting out have gone to arbitration in the absence of a specific governing clause in the agreement, the arbitrators have tended to favor the union if the outside contractor paid lower wages than were paid in the bargaining unit. Often, however, the outside contractor pays high wages,

[1] A recent thorough study of contracting out by manufacturing firms found that 32 per cent of the firms studied had provisions in their union agreements governing contracting out, and another 28 per cent of the firms had informal understandings with the union. See Margaret K. Chandler and Leonard R. Sayles, *Contracting Out* (Graduate School of Business, Columbia University, 1959), pp. 29–34.

perhaps to members of a craft union, and his advantage lies in having specialized knowledge and equipment, or specially skilled workers who can be furnished in large numbers for short periods. In such cases, the arbitration decisions have tended to favor management.

§ 6. **Increasing the Demand for the Product.** Many of the devices discussed above are ways of trying to increase employment for a given level of demand for the product. Some unions have tried instead to promote the use of their product, often in connection with efforts of employers. Sometimes the union conducts or participates in an advertising campaign, either for the product in general or for products bearing the union label in particular. It is doubtful whether these campaigns have any appreciable effect.

A union may also attempt to protect markets for its product by political activity or lobbying. For example, the United Mine Workers, along with coal mine operators and domestic petroleum producers, conducted a successful campaign for the limitation of imports of crude petroleum. This restriction helps to preserve employment in the coal mining industry and in the domestic production of crude petroleum, at the expense of consumers.

Unions of workers in industries facing severe competition from imports have generally favored import quotas or high tariffs. With the organization of industrial unions in many export industries in the 1930's and with the increasing liberalism of unions (in the usual American political sense) after that time, the position of the labor movement as a whole came to be in general one of favoring the lowering of barriers to international trade. Beginning in the late 1950's, increased competition from imports in a number of industries has caused several unions to retreat from a position of favoring free trade. There have even been one or two brief boycotts of foreign components and materials.

§ 7. **Hours of Work.** Because union regulation of the hours of work is ordinarily regarded as a major aspect of union activity in itself, it is unusual to discuss it in connection with union practices affecting productivity and employment. However, one purpose of limiting hours of work is to give employment to additional members of the union, and it may often be less efficient to add new employees than to work the regular employees overtime. The strongest evidence that union limitation of the hours of work is part of an effort to make jobs go around is the timing of reductions in the standard work week in unionized industries. The work week has frequently been shortened during depressions when there were many unemployed union members.

The early history of the shorter-hours movement is marked by frequent and convincing appeals that workers working as long as twelve hours a day had no leisure, no time to devote to their self-improvement, and no time to fulfil their duties as parents and citizens. As the work week has been shortened, such appeals are less frequently met.

Perhaps the most intriguing of the traditional union arguments for shorter hours is that very long hours reduce productivity so much that total output would be greater and costs would be lower if the hours were shortened. It is reasonable to suppose that there is some limit beyond which longer hours do not increase output, and there is experimental evidence supporting this position. It is also reasonable to suppose that this limit is not a fixed one, but depends in part on the hours to which workers are accustomed. Thus during World War II it may well have been true that hours of work in excess of 55 or 60 per week were self-defeating because they caused reductions in output per man-hour, increases in absenteeism and turnover, and reductions in the quality of output. It does not follow that the same was true at the turn of the century, when 60 hours was a common work week.

The puzzle is to see why employers would ever set hours so high that output would be reduced. It is possible for a particular employer so to misjudge his self-interest, but if others do not, the pressure of competition should force him into line. If employers as a group set hours that are too long in this absolute sense, any innovating employer who shortened hours would have a competitive advantage. The argument must depend on a combination of employer ignorance and a strong force of custom equalizing hours among employers. This combination is not impossible, though it does not seem likely.

In general unions do not set absolute limits on the hours of work. Rather they require higher rates of pay for work beyond the standard number of hours. Such extra pay is premium pay from the point of view of the worker, and penalty pay from the point of view of the employer. If the employer cannot avoid some overtime work, the effect of premium rates is simply to increase average hourly earnings. Where the employer can control hours to some extent, penalty rates will induce him to schedule less overtime.

Most unionized industries are subject to the Fair Labor Standards Act of 1938, which requires pay of time and one-half for work in excess of 40 hours per week for workers engaged in interstate commerce. In industries not subject to the act, similar overtime rates are usually set by collective bargaining. Within the area covered by the act, collective bargaining often imposes additional requirements, such as double pay for work on Sundays and holidays. Some unions have also negotiated shorter standard work weeks than are required by law; standard work weeks of 35 and 36 hours are reasonably common, especially in the printing, garment, building, and rubber industries.

Premium rates of time and one-half or double time are more than adequate to offset any natural disinclination to work overtime, with the result that opportunities for overtime work are eagerly sought and are usually allocated according to seniority. Under these circumstances, the employers and the junior workers (though not the senior workers) would be better off with a lower premium rate, at which the increased number of opportunities for overtime work and the reduced number of applicants for them would be roughly equal. The members of a union as a whole may benefit from high premium rates if the chance for overtime work is rotated among all the members.

§ 8. **Guarantees of Work to the Individual.** Manual workers have traditionally been paid by the hour. Management has been free to lay them off without pay whenever they have not been needed, even for part of a day, or to inform them that no work was available after they had reported to work. In contrast, most white-collar employees are paid a salary that continues even if there is little for them to do on a particular day. This distinction has been an important symbol of status for the salaried worker and correspondingly has been viewed as an injustice by manual workers and their unions. Although the distinction has by no means disappeared, many unions have negotiated call-in pay provisions that modify the traditional practices. Provisions of this kind often require that a worker who reports to work, having been given no advance notice that work was not available, must receive a minimum of half a day's pay even if he does not work, or works less than half a day. Such a provision is of considerable value to workers, and does not impose substantial costs on employers, since the necessity for call-in pay can usually be averted by a minimum of advance planning.

Immediately following World War II, a great deal was written about a much more sweeping guarantee of work to the individual, the guaranteed annual wage. Such plans are in effect in a few establishments; the most widely cited is the plan negotiated by the United Packinghouse Workers and the Hormel Packing Company. The plans provide that a worker is guaranteed a minimum number of hours of work or pay per year, usually two thousand hours. In return, the employer is given unusual freedom to transfer employees among jobs and is relieved of the requirement to pay overtime premiums for work in excess of 40 hours a week. A special provision of the Fair Labor Standards Act permits an exemption from its overtime pay requirements when such a plan is in effect.

Union attempts to extend the guaranteed annual wage on a

large scale were successfully resisted by employers on the grounds that it would be excessively costly. Many industries with large seasonal or cyclical fluctuations in employment have felt that they could not provide steady work and that the plans would require large payments for time not worked. Since 1955 several large unions, especially the automobile workers and the steelworkers, have negotiated supplementary unemployment benefit (SUB) instead of the guaranteed annual wage. The SUB plans do not guarantee work to anyone but instead provide a partial guarantee of income during layoffs in addition to that provided by unemployment insurance. The typical SUB plan will increase a worker's income during a layoff from about 40 or 45 per cent of his basic pay after taxes, which is the range most often provided by unemployment insurance laws, to 60 or 65 per cent. In addition, the SUB plan may pay the full 60 or 65 per cent of base take-home pay to workers whose rights to unemployment insurance have been exhausted. The typical unemployment insurance law provides only 26 weeks of benefits; some SUB plans provide up to 52.

By contributing to the maintenance of incomes during a recession, SUB plans reduce the curtailment of spending by the unemployed and thus make it less likely that unemployment will become cumulative. Because SUB plans specify benefits in terms of a total of public and supplementary benefits combined, with the SUB plan making up the difference between the public benefits and the total, the plans have undoubtedly reduced employer opposition to higher benefits in state unemployment insurance laws and thus have contributed to the liberalization of benefits for workers outside the unions concerned.

Supplementary unemployment benefits are financed by specified employer contributions to a benefit fund, and the employer is not liable to pay benefits that cannot be paid from the balance in the fund. To conserve the fund, benefits are restricted to senior employees or are sharply curtailed for others when the fund is low. In principle, the existence of supplementary unemployment insurance benefits could make employers reluctant to hire new employees or could make unemployed workers less willing to look for work. There is little reason to suppose that either effect has been of any appreciable importance. The premium for overtime is so much higher than the rate of contribution for SUB that it is still cheaper for employers covered by SUB to hire additional employees than to pay for large amounts of overtime. The difference between the total income of unemployed workers and of employed workers remains large enough under SUB plans to provide a substantial incentive for prompt return to work. Moreover, workers who do not report to work when recalled may lose precious seniority and pension rights. A possible effect of SUB on the employment of the unemployed may be to reduce the tendency to take temporary odd jobs, but these are seldom available in any substantial number in a steel or auto manufacturing town during a period of layoffs.

Many unions also have won special provisions for workers displaced by technological changes and permanent shutdowns of plants or other facilities. These include lump-sum severance pay and rights to transfer to other plants. Recently, the parties to a few collective bargaining agreements have begun to experiment with retraining programs for permanently displaced workers. Transfer or retraining programs are likely to be of more lasting benefit to the worker than severance pay, for when this is gone he may still be unemployed or employed only at a low skill level. However, transfer programs create a substantial internal problem for the union. When a company shuts one of several plants and it is proposed that workers be transferred to the remaining plants, the local unions in the receiving plants may object strenuously. Often the best that can be done is to give the displaced workers preferential hiring rights at other plants without displacing any of the workers presently employed there.

CHAPTER VIII

SENIORITY

§ 1. The Uses of Seniority. Almost all collective agreements provide that seniority shall govern layoffs. Within the defined seniority unit, the oldest employee in point of service is the last laid off and the first rehired, except that superseniority is sometimes given to the union steward or committeeman. A union may prefer work-sharing to layoffs as a way of dealing with moderate decreases in the amount of work needed, but beyond some point (when the workweek has been reduced to, say, 30 hours) layoffs ordinarily occur and seniority governs their order. The use of seniority in layoffs has spread to many non-union plants and may even be formalized into non-union seniority systems.

The use of seniority in promotions within the non-supervisory workforce is also widespread, though it is usually modified by some consideration of ability. For example, it may be provided that the senior employee shall have the first trial at a job opening in a higher pay category, but that he may be replaced by the next senior if he fails to do satisfactory work during a trial period. A disagreement over the adequacy of his performance could be adjudicated through the grievance procedure. A less typical provision would be that seniority governs promotion where ability is equal; this kind of provision gives management more discretionary power.

Finally, seniority is often used to govern work assignments of various sorts. The senior employee may have the first chance to work overtime or the junior employee may be

151

required to work night shifts. In operating occupations on the railroads and airlines, seniority usually governs the choice of runs or flights; this choice is often an important determinant of individual earnings.

§ 2. **The Reasons for Seniority.** Seniority appeals to a widespread feeling of what is fair: the rule of "first come, first served" or the "ethics of the queue."[1] It thus serves as a way of allocation or ordering in many situations where price allocation is inappropriate or inconvenient. These include situations far removed from unions, such as the seating of ambassadors at a state dinner, the listing of faculty names in a university catalogue, or the succession to the desk by the window in a non-union office. This notion of fairness is probably a more important basis for seniority systems than any notion of respect for the older workers, since respect for the aged is not a very strong characteristic of American culture.

At heart, a seniority system is designed to prevent favoritism by foremen in the making of layoffs, promotions, and work assignments. It therefore creates vested rights in jobs which were once held at the pleasure of supervisors. Workers' stories of the pre-union period stress over and over again that one had to do favors for the foreman to hold a job—flatter him, buy him drinks, even paint his porch. This folklore undoubtedly contains an element of exaggeration, but it also contains an element of truth.

Why should there have been favoritism or abuse of authority in the pre-union situation? The worker view seems to be that this is characteristic of the personality of people who accept jobs as foremen or of what the job does to them. Foremen are or become people who revel in the exercise of authority and in demonstrating superiority to ordinary workers. For this reason a worker with strong ties to the work group will often say that he would not want to be a foreman.

[1] See Melvin W. Reder, "Job Scarcity and the Nature of Union Power," *Industrial and Labor Relations Review*, April, 1960, pp. 353–57.

Without wholly denying the relevance of such psychological explanations, one can also explain favoritism along economic lines. The downward inflexibility of wages and the instability of the demand for labor in many industries created frequent periods of excess labor supply in the pre-union era. Firms therefore had to ration jobs among applicants or among their workers. They did not want to use price rationing; this would have required substantial wage cuts that would have seemed unfair to workers and to the public and that could have stimulated the organization of unions. The idea of using seniority in layoffs seems not to have occurred to employers of manual labor. In the absence of any other device, the foreman was left free to use his own criteria. If the career incentives for running an efficient shop were great enough, he could lay off the least able workers first, according to his own assessment of ability. Or he could use his power to increase his personal satisfaction, through graft or favoritism. Oddly enough, this situation so hated by the industrial unionist is basically the same situation that creates favoritism in the choice of entrants to closed-shop unions.

The principle of seniority in layoffs is seldom questioned by employers today. Presumably, the costs have been small, or have been borne by the foremen or by the junior workers rather'than by the firm. The application of the principle can nevertheless give rise to difficult problems.

§ 3. The Seniority Unit. The size and nature of the seniority unit have an important bearing on the degree of protection offered by a seniority system and on the costs of the system to management. Seniority can be company-wide, plant-wide, or departmental. In some industries, it extends across companies and is market-wide for certain occupations. And within any of these scopes, it can be confined within specified occupations, or it can extend to permit a man to displace a junior man in any occupation of lesser skill. The wider the seniority unit, the greater the protection against layoff given the senior employee and the greater the dislocation that can be caused by a single layoff. Suppose, for example, there is plant-wide seniority for machinists in a plant that employs many machinists in a variety of departments. A certain department lays off a machinist with five years' seniority. He can then displace or "bump" any machinist with less seniority in any other department. This man in turn can bump any man junior to him, each man selecting the place where the reduction in his earnings or the worsening of his working conditions is least. Several transfers of workers among departments may be required before the process terminates and some junior machinist is actually laid off. These transfers will usually involve both learning costs and record-keeping costs. To avoid such costs, management tries to keep the seniority units narrow. In most cases workable compromises are arrived at over a period of years, involving a reasonable degree of protection and reasonable freedom from long chains of transfers.

Special problems sometimes put the logic of seniority units to severe tests. In a plant where departmental seniority is in force, a department might be permanently abolished. Men with many years' seniority would be discharged while new employees stayed on the job in other departments. The other departments, however, would probably resist a change to plant-wide seniority. Often a compromise solution can be reached; for example, a man might be allowed to carry half his original departmental seniority into another department. Such problems are essentially internal problems of job allocation within the union; management may have much less interest in the nature of the final compromise than the workers do.

§ 4. **Seniority and Efficiency.** The principle of seniority seems to conflict strongly with efficiency, with the selection or retention of the most able or productive man for each job. There is undoubtedly some conflict, though there is less than one might think for several reasons. First, there is a natural positive correlation between productivity and experience.

Second, the seniority system did not replace selection by measured ability; as we have seen, it replaced a system of subjective selection that had important elements of favoritism and guessing. In many areas it is doubtful whether employers have reliable measures of ability. Third, where a worker has leadership ability as contrasted with mechanical ability, there are two natural outlets for his talents that lie outside of the seniority system. One is election or appointment to union office, the other is promotion to a supervisory position. Suitable men are often hard to find for positions of either type. Finally, as mentioned above, seniority in promotion is usually qualified by some reference to ability or merit.

A fifth factor is sometimes mentioned as reducing the conflict between seniority and efficiency; it is said that a seniority system makes management select employees more carefully and with a view to their future promotion. Although the assertion may well be true, it does not follow that such practices avoid the costs of seniority in promotions; they may merely alter the form that these costs take. Under old hiring standards, the cost would be the promotion of poorly qualified men. Under the new standards, the costs are the higher starting wages needed to get new workers all of whom have potential for promotion. The use of exceptionally able men as laborers because they will one day be eligible for promotion to skilled jobs involves an uneconomic reduction in the specialization of labor.

The use of seniority to govern work assignments, such as the assignment of men to shifts, also involves inefficiency. This inefficiency could presumably be corrected by setting up a better system of premium pay. In almost all industries, senior employees choose to work day shifts, which suggests that the premium for night work is too low. The aversion to working at night may be correlated with age, and thus with seniority. However, if it varies randomly among workers, then the distribution of workers by shifts should also be uncorrelated with seniority. At the "right" night-shift premium, enough workers would prefer to work nights to fill the available openings in the night shift. Some of these workers who would then prefer night work would be senior employees, and new employees would no longer need to be required to start on the night shift if they did not choose to. This would presumably improve the ability of the firm to attract qualified workers. In order to guarantee that the firm gains from the change, we must specify that the average earnings do not change; that is the premium is created by lowering day-shift rates as well as raising night-shift rates. This would be hard to negotiate. However, when a general wage increase had been agreed on, the firm might gain from specifying that some of it be used to widen shift differentials. In the similar case of overtime premiums, it was noted in the last chapter that identical reasoning suggests they are now too large.

§ 5. **Seniority and Mobility.** It is widely and no doubt correctly assumed that the use of seniority to govern layoffs and promotions has contributed to the secular decrease in the voluntary mobility of American manual labor. Experimental evidence on the point is difficult to find. Senior employees will on the average tend to be older than junior employees in any work group, and we know from many studies that mobility declines with age. We have no good measures of the size of the decline in mobility with seniority when age is held constant. In addition to seniority, there are other aspects of the employment relation, such as the presence of non-vested pensions, that should also tend to reduce mobility, and some of these may be more common in union than in non-union situations.

The reduction in voluntary quits brought about by seniority and non-vested pensions is valuable to the employer, because quits involve him in hiring and training costs for new employees. This may be one of the reasons that seniority systems, though usually introduced by unions, have seldom been strongly opposed by employers. The savings to individual employers from reduced quit rates will not necessarily be beneficial to the economy unless they are needed to induce the employer to train his workers. Reduced voluntary mobility can slow the adjustment of employment to changes in demand and increase the wages that must be offered by new and expanding employments to secure enough qualified employees.

The stress that has been put on seniority and on grievance procedures as protection of the rights of individual workers has unfortunately tended to obscure the fact that the possibility of easy movement—that is, a smoothly functioning labor market—is also an important source of protection. Under conditions of full employment, a worker can often escape dissatisfactions by changing jobs, provided that the institutions of the market make it possible for him to start with a new employer at a level that reflects the value of his accumulated skills. The protection offered by mobility is protection not only against any arbitrary exercise of power by the employer, but also against any unfairness toward the individual member by a particular local union, or by a national union if there is more than one having jurisdiction over his line of work.

In the years since World War II, the protection offered by the market has probably been inherently greater than ever before. The level of employment has on the whole been reasonably high. Workers have had more liquid assets than before to tide them over the period following a voluntary quit. The widespread ownership of cars has facilitated both changes in residence and changes in place of work without change in residence. The rising education of workers and the existence of government employment services should have increased the level of knowledge of alternative job opportunities. Despite all this, the level of quit rates has been falling.

The spread of seniority systems seems to be a major factor in the reduction in voluntary quits and in the increasing difficulties faced by displaced workers past the age of 45 in finding new jobs that use their experience. Even where seniority governs layoffs, some long-service workers do lose their jobs because of shifts in demand, changes in technology, and the business failure of employers. Such workers can get new work readily at their old skill level only if their skill is high, scarce, and easily transferable—for example, if they are tool- and die-makers. Most displaced workers must start their new employment not only at the bottom of the seniority list, but at the bottom of the skill ladder. Often they must start in a common labor pool and slowly work their way back up the channels of promotion from within. Clearly, this situation both discourages quits and unfairly penalizes those who have the misfortune to be displaced. The loss to the worker under discussion here is not the loss involved when his skills are no longer needed by anyone, though this too is a serious problem. The loss to workers from obsolescence of skills is an especially severe form of the loss from an investment that turns out badly. However, the situation created by the widespread use of seniority in promotion goes beyond this, for it imposes losses on the worker whose skills are still valuable to many employers, but who cannot get the chance to use them.

Because of the high value placed by most workers and unions on the protection offered by seniority systems, it does not seem possible to solve the problem just posed by any large-scale abandonment of the use of seniority in promotion. The development of multiemployer seniority units may be a partial solution in some industries, especially those having many employers in the same locality. As improved methods are developed for the objective evaluation of experience and skill, unions may come to permit somewhat more hiring from the outside at upper skill levels than is now typical. This hope, however, has often been expressed in the past and there is as yet little sign of its fulfilment.

CHAPTER IX

GRIEVANCE PROCEDURES

§ 1. The Changed Status of the Industrial Worker. The remaining sections of this chapter describe the operation of grievance procedures established by collective bargaining. Such a description, however, fails to convey the full impact of grievance machinery and related union practices on the status of the industrial worker. As an introduction to the more specific discussion, this section will attempt to summarize the effect of these institutional changes on the worker's position in the social system of the work place.

In the pre-union period, the manual worker in large-scale industry was separated by a wide gulf from management and from the white-collar work force. (I have deliberately written of the pre-union period rather than the non-union plant, because the changes under discussion have also occurred in non-union plants, in part as a result of the threat of unionization, in part as a result of new management attitudes and mores, and in part as a result of the rising educational and income levels of industrial workers.) One of the first qualities expected of the worker before unionization was unquestioning obedience. The disciplinary code of the factory and mine included a grave offense called insubordination, which suggests the authoritarian nature of the relation between worker and supervisor. The power to discipline, including the power to suspend or discharge a worker, rested in the foreman, and there was rarely any effective channel of appeal from his decision.

159

Although the nature of industrial discipline is perhaps the most conspicuous mark of the old status gulf, there were many others. As recently as 1929, wages were considerably lower relative to salaries than they are today. Paid vacations, paid holidays, and pensions existed for salaried workers long before they spread to wage-earners. Even in the location and quality of their homes and in other aspects of consumption, manual workers were more sharply set apart from white-collar workers than they are today. Some managers were indifferent to the living conditions and working conditions of wage-earners, while others took a sincere paternalistic interest in improving them, but in neither case would it have occurred to them that the industrial worker should have a voice in the determination of his own working conditions. This attitude was made easier because so many of the industrial workers and relatively few of the managers of forty or fifty years ago were immigrants. The managers could tell themselves that the workers were by culture and nature suited to thrive on conditions that they themselves would have found intolerable.

Today, the difference in status between manual workers and white-collar workers in the United States is probably the smallest in the world, with little more than the blue denim shirt and the hourly wage remaining to distinguish the operative from his white-collar neighbor. The union has contributed to this change in many ways. The control of layoffs through seniority systems and the control of discipline through grievance procedures are perhaps the most important of these. Union activities have also brought changes within management, leading it to devote much more attention to the personnel function and to give greater weight to worker sentiment and attitudes in its planning. Personnel and industrial relations departments have grown tremendously, and their directors occupy much higher places in the corporate hierarchy. The foreman's right to discipline has been severely restricted, so that in most cases he merely initiates disciplinary action, which is not made effective except with the approval of higher levels of management.

Almost every worker old enough to remember the pre-union period treasures some story of what this change in status has meant to him.   For example, one of the leading automobile companies had a rule for many years that only cars of its own manufacture could be parked on company parking lots.   One of the early actions of the union when it was recognized as a bargaining agent was to insist that this rule be rescinded. Many workers seemed to value this symbolic increase in their personal freedom more than any other union accomplishment.

§ 2. **Types of Grievance Procedures.**   A grievance is a complaint by a worker that he has not been treated fairly in some aspect of his work or pay, usually in an aspect specifically covered by the collective agreement.   There is great variation in the nature of the complaints, though certain complaints recur frequently.   Among these are grievances about rates of pay (for example, a worker may feel that the work he has been doing should be classified as carrying a higher rate than he is receiving).   Seniority grievances are also common; a worker alleges that if his seniority had been reckoned properly, he would have been promoted or transferred to a more desirable position instead of someone else.   The grievance machinery is also frequently used to protest discipline that is considered unwarranted or unduly severe.

Where unions bargain with small employers the grievance system is often very simple.   The worker makes his complaint orally to his immediate supervisor; if he does not get satisfaction, he goes to the union president or business agent, who talks to the owner or manager of the firm.   Such an informal procedure is clearly unworkable in large companies, where elaborate formal systems of handling grievances have evolved. In such systems the worker goes in the first instance to his shop steward, an elected part-time union official sometimes called a grievance committeeman or a "griever."   If the steward feels that the grievance is a legitimate one, he will help the worker to put it in writing and will try to settle it with the foreman. The requirement that a grievance be put in writing causes a surprising number of complaints to evaporate at this point. If the grievance cannot be settled between the steward and the foreman, it will proceed upward through a well-defined series of steps involving increasingly higher levels of authority within the union and the management. A typical procedure in a large firm might involve as a second step a conference between an officer of the local union (sometimes called the chief steward) and the plant personnel department. As a third step, if necessary, there might be a meeting between the grievance committee of the local union and a committee from the plant management. If this formal deliberation failed to dispose of the issue, the next step might move it away from the plant level and it would be presented to the personnel department of the company at its headquarters by an international representative of the union. As a final step, the great majority of grievance procedures provide for neutral arbitration.

Grievance procedures have been developed to an unusually high level by American unions, particularly industrial unions. In contrast, in many European countries such issues are not handled by unions at all but by plant committees that represent members of several unions and of none. The grievance procedure has tended to keep unions in close touch with their members and to maintain life and interest in the local union by giving it an important function. The protection offered by a well-operating grievance procedure is particularly important in discipline cases, since the growth of pension and seniority rights has made discharge for cause an increasingly severe penalty even when there is full employment. The grievance procedure has become a full-fledged system of industrial jurisprudence, responsive to local pressures at the bottom and responsible to a neutral but specialized judiciary at the top. The shop steward occupies a particularly important place in this system, for he is the direct representative of the worker to management and of the union to the worker. He is paid for the time he spends in handling grievances at his ordinary rate of pay as a worker, under some agreements by management and under others by the union. In large plants, a steward may spend most or all of his time in his union duties, and little if any on the work to which he is nominally assigned by the company.

In order for a union to participate in a successful grievance procedure, it is not necessary for it to have any appreciable power to raise wages. It is true that there are costs to such a procedure—the time spent by workers and management in handling grievances, the costs of arbitration, and the cost of concessions won for workers in grievance settlements. The power to impose these costs on management is implied in the union's ability to become a recognized bargaining agent and to negotiate a contract including grievance provisions. However, these are not necessarily net costs, since a good grievance procedure can help to improve productivity and reduce labor turnover. Moreover, some of the costs are paid for by union members through their dues. The existence of formal grievance systems in non-union firms seems to demonstrate that such systems can be of benefit to management as well as to workers, though many managements would not have believed this possible until it had been tried. The lack of a necessary relationship between economic power and union ability to help members in their day-to-day problems may explain in part the continued strength (as measured by size of membership and member loyalty) of some unions, like that in the men's clothing industry, which no longer seem to have any appreciable economic power. Conversely, some unions with considerable power over wages put little emphasis on handling grievances.

§ 3. The Arbitration of Grievances. Several different kinds of arbitration of grievances are provided in collective agreements. The arbitration may be by a tripartite board consisting of representatives of the union, the management, and a neutral. More frequently, a neutral is the sole arbitrator. In a small company where few cases go to arbitration, a new arbitrator may be selected for each case. In large companies, a permanent arbitrator or umpire is usually selected to hear all cases until one of the parties asks that he be removed. Permanent arbitrators are also used in some agreements covering many small firms. Despite the fact that permanent arbitrators serve at the pleasure of the parties and must constantly make decisions that disappoint one side or the other, many have had a surprisingly long tenure. Most arbitrators are lawyers, though labor economists, sociologists, and even philosophers and clergymen have often been used. Labor arbitrators often combine their arbitration with legal practice or with teaching, though a number of the most prominent men in the field make labor arbitration a full-time career. Arbitrators are selected by agreement between the parties; special provision is usually made for a method of selection in the event that the parties are unable to agree. The costs of arbitration are shared by the parties.

The role that the arbitrator is expected to play differs considerably depending on the nature of the bargaining relationship. In long-established and friendly bargaining relationships where there is full acceptance of the union by management, the arbitrator may be a "problem-solver." The parties come to him with any sort of difficulty that they are unable to resolve, whether or not it is covered by the agreement. The arbitrator is then free to propose solutions based on his knowledge of the industry and the bargaining relation; in effect he is a mediator as well as an arbitrator. In other cases, and especially where the bargaining relation is new or unfriendly, the role of the arbitrator will be more restricted. He will be confined to interpreting the agreement and will be expected to support his findings by references to specific contract provisions. If a rather literal reading of the agreement creates severe problems for one of the parties, it can bargain for revision of the relevant provisions when the agreement expires; in the meantime it must live with them as best it can. Arm's length bargaining relationships tend to develop complex and detailed agreements; because these will often be interpreted by arbitrators with legal training, they will usually be drafted by attorneys for the parties. Arbitration decisions often set precedents that control many cases other than the one actually arbitrated; however, the application of precedent and of case law is not as rigid in arbitration as in civil or criminal law.

In most jurisdictions, the findings of a voluntary arbitration are not binding on the parties. There have nevertheless been very few cases in which a union or a management has refused to give effect to an arbitration decision. Such an action by management would, of course, be an invitation to a strike.

The fact that an arbitrator of a grievance under an existing agreement can turn to the agreement for guidance makes the arbitration of grievances very different from the arbitration of disputes over the terms of new agreements. In the latter case, there are no agreed criteria for the arbitrators and they have a strong tendency to compromise between the positions of the parties. This is particularly true in wage arbitrations, which frequently "split the difference." In grievance arbitrations, however, arbitrators can and frequently do find one party or the other wholly in the wrong.

§ 4. The Well-Functioning Grievance Procedure.

It might be thought that a well-functioning grievance procedure is one that has few grievances to process. Actually, a procedure to which no grievances are submitted is probably working very badly indeed. In any work situation involving many people there are bound to be problems and controversies. In a well-functioning grievance machinery these will lead to the filing of a considerable number of grievances, most of which will be disposed of in the early steps of the procedure leaving very few to be negotiated at higher levels or to be arbitrated. If few grievances are ever filed, this probably indicates that the workers have lost confidence in the procedure and are finding other outlets for their dissatisfactions. This loss of confidence could arise because the union was discouraging or refusing to process legitimate grievances, or because settlements of grievances were long delayed. A good grievance procedure disposes of the great majority of grievances promptly while they are still relevant.

At the other extreme, a grievance procedure in which very few complaints can be settled at the lower levels and many are carried through to arbitration is also not working well. Such a situation indicates a hostile union-management relationship in which every grievance is seen not as a problem to be solved equitably but as a skirmish in a struggle between union and management for power or for worker loyalty.

One evidence of a badly functioning grievance procedure would be frequent resort by workers to slowdowns, wildcat strikes, and other direct devices for the expression of dissatisfaction. At the individual level, this could take the form of high quit rates or excessive absenteeism. In such cases the resentment of the worker need not be directed at management; it can also be directed at a union that is falling down on the job. Of course, even a good grievance procedure will not necessarily avert all wildcat strikes or slowdowns. The formal settlement of grievances once they get beyond the first step inevitably takes some time, and sometimes a work group will feel that its problems are too pressing to permit any delay. Threats or fancied threats to the health and safety of workers are among the problems that may lead to this kind of shortcutting of established channels even in a good bargaining relationship.

A good grievance procedure can be of help to top management in detecting trouble spots at lower levels in its own organization. Upward communication in a formal hierarchy can be highly selective, with subordinates tending to suppress information that might reflect on their own performance. The grievance procedure tends to short-circuit this biased system of communication. It is by no means unheard of for a foreman to encourage a worker to file a grievance as a way of making a problem known to someone in management above the level of his own superior.

A number of non-union firms have established grievance procedures, and some of these seem to function effectively. The personnel department of a non-union company can in effect represent individual workers in disputes with line management. However, the non-union grievance procedure rarely has neutral arbitration as a last step. The role of even the most worker-oriented personnel man is an ambiguous one; he must feel a divided loyalty as between the worker and the firm that would not be felt by a union representative. For this reason, unions seem to have a strong relative advantage in the handling of grievances, especially in the large firm where internal communication in management becomes slow and difficult, and top management is far removed from the work place. There are, however, a few conspicuous examples of large non-union employers of manual labor whose labor relations are so good that the workers have repeatedly voted down unions in free elections.

It is less clear whether the local independent union is at a disadvantage in grievance settlement relative to the national union. The independent may in some cases be able to keep in closer touch with a situation than a national union, where grievance settlement is taken out of the hands of local people at higher steps in the procedure. On the other hand, the national union has greater resources in terms of specialized personnel in such areas as legal counsel and industrial engineering, and the hired or retained outsider sometimes used by independent unions cannot always provide equal *expertise*. Some of the effectiveness of local independent unions in handling grievances may depend on an implicit threat that they will affiliate with a national union if reasonable complaints are seldom remedied.

§ 5. **Shortcomings in Grievance Procedures.** On the whole, we must regard the grievance procedure as it has evolved in American industrial relations as a highly successful and desirable institution. However, even highly successful institutions develop flaws, and in this respect grievance machinery is no exception. The brief listing below suggests some of the problem areas.

There may be some individuals within the bargaining unit who cannot get their grievances processed or get them pushed with sufficient vigor.   If there is no union shop, this may be true of workers who are not members of the union.   Although the union has an obligation to process grievances for non-members, this obligation is not always adequately discharged. The non-member also has the right to present his own grievances if the union representative is present (the union wants to make sure that any concessions made to the non-member do not adversely affect the interests of any members). However, management may be influenced in settling these complaints by the need for maintaining good relations with the union.   Within the union membership itself there may also be individuals who have difficulty in getting adequate represen-tation, perhaps because of color, national origin, or minority political position within the union.   Unions reserve the right to refuse to process grievances that in their judgment have no merit.   This reservation is needed to prevent the grievance machinery from getting clogged with groundless complaints. But if the worker cannot be persuaded that his complaint is groundless, and the union cannot be persuaded to put it forward, his grievance has in effect been transformed into a grievance against the union.   A few unions have adequate internal appeals machinery for considering these complaints at higher levels within the union; in two cases, the upholsterers and the automobile workers, these internal appeals procedures terminate at the highest step in a board of neutral outsiders. In many other unions, however, internal appeals procedures are inadequate or lacking.   Even when a member eventually wins an appeal within the union, this favorable decision may not be reached until long after the time limit for filing a grievance with management has passed.

A special problem is created by the logrolling of grievances, a mode of settling two difficult cases, one in favor of the aggrieved in return for one in favor of management.   If both grievances have merit, the result is more symmetrical than just. Every union manual for stewards and local union officers warns against this kind of settlement, but the temptation to dispose of issues this way may sometimes prove irresistible.

Some arbitrators have been worried by a problem that is perhaps not so closely related to grievance procedures as such as to the standards of punishment for offenses committed at work. In some firms, the penalty for such offenses as fighting on company premises, striking a foreman, or reporting for work drunk is dismissal. Under modern conditions in which seniority and pension rights are built up over long periods and employers are reluctant to hire older workers, this penalty may be much more severe than the penalties for corresponding offenses in the community at large. Yet the union role in discipline cases, like that of the neutral arbitrator, may be confined to questioning whether the man actually committed the offense. If it is clear that he did, the union may not be able to mitigate the penalty. On the other hand, the severity of discharge under these conditions may restrain management from using it even for very serious offenses, and this may contribute to the weakening of discipline.

CHAPTER X

THE UNION AS A POLITICAL INSTITUTION

§ 1. The General Nature of Union Government. Since this is primarily a book about the economics of trade unions, a chapter on politics may seem out of place. However, the political character of unions so permeates everything they do, including their economic activities, that the book would be seriously incomplete without some explicit consideration of union politics.

At first glance, union government looks very like civil government in a democracy. In both, the administrative functions are directed by elected officials, and the convention of a national union is roughly analogous to a legislature. The frequent use by unions of the terms and symbols of democracy also contributes to this first impression. Nevertheless, the impression is misleading and the differences between union government and government in the larger body politic are more important than the formal similarities.

American political democracy rests on at least three major principles. The first is majority rule in the election of officials and in the making of decisions in the legislative bodies. The second is the guarantee and general recognition of the rights of minorities. The third, closely related to the second, is the recognition of the legitimacy of organized opposition; today's minority has the undisputed right to try to become tomorrow's majority. Of these three principles, the first is formally recognized by all national unions and actually practiced by most. However, it may be largely empty without

the remaining two, and these are seldom present.   Only a few
national unions have strong guarantees of the rights of
minorities, and only one, the International Typographical
Union, has a functioning two-party system and recognizes the
legitimacy of organized opposition.[1]

If unions are regarded as voluntary organizations, this
absence of fully functioning democracy can be considered
both natural and unimportant.   It has long been recognized
that most voluntary organizations are controlled by their
officers and staffs and that very few contain oppositions
except on a transitory basis.   In particular, the democratic
forms observed in the government of corporations seldom have
enough vitality to permit stockholders to overturn a corporate
management in a proxy battle.   These comparisons, however,
are not as consoling as they might be.   First, a union is not
entirely a voluntary organization.   Many members are   (1)
required by union shop contracts to maintain their membership
or lose their jobs.   Even where membership is voluntary, the
fact that a union is a recognized bargaining agent means that
it continues to make decisions that affect the conditions under
which the non-members earn their living.   In contrast the
typical voluntary organization affects a much smaller and less
important part of the lives of its members.   In a corporation,
the disgruntled minority stockholder can usually sell his
shares at a fair price.   Although the right of the union member
to change jobs is formally similar to the right of the minority
stockholder to sell his shares, the costs to the union member
of leaving his job will usually be much greater.

A second reason for taking a more serious view of the
absence of full democracy in unions than in corporations is   (2)
that unions much more than businesses have made belief in
democracy a leading feature of their ideology.   Businessmen
usually assume that those who by their industry and thrift
have accumulated wealth or reached executive positions have

---

[1] The definitive study of the two-party system in the ITU is S. M.
Lipset, M. A. Trow, and J. S. Coleman, *Union Democracy* (Glencoe, Ill.:
Free Press, 1956).

earned the right to a controlling voice in corporate decisions. This view seems immoral to many unionists, who maintain that each individual should have an equal voice. Yet in fact, the concentration of decision-making power may be as great in unions as in corporations. This is true even in unions like the United Automobile Workers, where the dedication of the leaders to democracy is beyond question, and where the early history of the organization gave great promise of vigorous internal democracy. The logic of the development of national unions seems to override all such promise and good intentions.

The Landrum-Griffin Act contains a number of provisions that require unions to follow democratic practices in their internal government. It requires that every union member have an equal vote in elections and referendums, which was not always the case in the past—for example, some unions of skilled craftsmen have extended their jurisdictions to less skilled workers and given them inferior voting rights. The law also requires the regular holding of elections of officers, provides that elections be by secret ballot, and guarantees the rights of members to speak in union meetings and to assemble for exchanging views. This last provision may require the alteration of union constitutions with sweeping bans on "dual unionism."[1] The provisions on voting rights and elections will affect only a small minority of unions whose previous practices did not meet the standards of the act. Since the effects of the Landrum-Griffin Act on union government are not yet clear, most of the discussion of this chapter does not take its impact into account.

The remaining sections of this chapter will discuss some of the factors in the development of oligarchic union government. A few general considerations will be noted at this point. The struggle against communism in the American labor movement has had an important adverse effect on union democracy.

---

[1] For a more detailed discussion of these provisions of the act, see Philip Taft, "The Impact of Landrum-Griffin on Union Government," *Annals of the American Academy of Political and Social Science*, January, 1961.

Since Communists are not willing to abide by the rules of the democratic game except where it suits them, their opponents have often felt forced to take measures that run counter to these rules. Although the present influence of Communists in most unions is negligible, the suspicion of Communist influence still causes many kinds of internal opposition to be viewed with great alarm. The fact that unions are always (B) engaged to a greater or lesser extent in a struggle with employers also causes internal opposition to be suspect. It is argued that opposition, however well intentioned, gives support and comfort to employers who are trying to weaken the union. A very similar set of circumstances contributes to the coexistence of democratic forms and anti-democratic practices in Communist national governments, which can always argue that internal opposition is counterrevolutionary and gives comfort to capitalist enemies. (This comparison, needless to say, is an odious one to anti-Communist leaders of American unions.)

§ 2. Participation in Unions.

In unions, as in many other organizations, the participation of members in business meetings is typically very low. In large locals of industrial unions, it is often as low as 1 per cent of the membership. In smaller locals, the percentage of active participants may be higher, particularly if the union meeting serves an important social function. Thus in craft unions where members work on scattered jobs throughout a large area, the union meeting is an important place to renew old friendships.[1]

There are a number of reasons for this low rate of participation, despite the efforts of many local unions to increase attendance through such devices as combining business meetings with social programs. In large part, the low (1) attendance may simply reflect satisfaction with the way in which union affairs are being conducted. If things are going

[1] See J. Seidman, J. London, B. Karsh, and D. L. Tagliacozzo, *The Worker Views His Union* (Chicago: University of Chicago Press, 1958), Chapter IX.

well, why give up an evening at home to travel back to a shabby union hall near the plant and participate in a dull meeting? If this is the dominant reason, then low attendance does not mean that union decisions fail to reflect the will of the majority. In part, however, the apathy of many union members results from the fact that they cannot participate in important decisions even if they attend meetings. Lipset, Trow, and Coleman point out that attendance is relatively high in the ITU in part because the two-party system makes for spirited debate and close decisions. In many other unions the important decisions are made by the well-entrenched officials of the national union, and the business at local meetings is routine. This is less likely to be true where collective bargaining takes place at the local rather than the national level. Local unions frequently have vigorous democracy and spirited participation in meetings, even though their national union is a one-party union. Turnover in office is also much higher at the local level, in part because many local offices are unpaid and may represent more of a burden than a reward to the incumbents.

The level of education of union members also has a bearing on the level of participation. The work and training of typographers, musicians, and actors prepares them better for taking part in union affairs than that of hodcarriers or steel-workers.

§ 3. Relations Between National and Local Unions. The center of political power in the American trade union movement has long been the national union. The tendency for power to be concentrated at the national level was evident as early as the last part of the nineteenth century.[1] The political dominance of the national union is often a result of its economic role. Where a union bargains with such large multiplant corporations as General Motors or United States Steel, the concentration of major collective bargaining functions

---

[1] See Lloyd Ulman, *The Rise of the National Trade Union* (Cambridge, Mass.: Harvard University Press, 1955).

at the national level inevitably leaves little room for local autonomy. The same is true for unions that engage in national industry-wide bargaining with many firms. Where bargaining is decentralized, there is more independence for the large locals, but small locals with no full-time staff are still often highly dependent on the aid of the international representative in bargaining.

In most unions the right to authorize strikes is reserved to the national union. Individual locals cannot build up the funds needed to pay strike benefits, and where such funds exist they are usually administered nationally. The requirement that strikes be authorized by the national union is intended to prevent the dissipation of strike funds in futile battles and to prevent hot-headed action from injuring the reputation of the national union.

The national union also has the right in most cases to suspend the charter of a local or to put it under trusteeship. A trustee is appointed by the national union to administer the affairs of a local if there is evidence of mismanagement. In many unions, trusteeship is used only where there is a strong case that the local has not handled its affairs with competence or honesty, and the trusteeship is ended as soon as possible. In some cases, however, locals have been put under trusteeship for essentially political reasons—that is, because local leaders have opposed or challenged the national administration. Some such trusteeships have continued for many years. The Landrum-Griffin Act of 1959 contains provisions restricting the rights of national unions to place their locals under trusteeship. It is too soon to say what the effects of this regulation will be.

§ 4. The Union Officer and His Staff.
The top officers of national unions are usually men who have begun as workers in the trade and have worked their way upward through the union hierarchy. A few national unions have presidents who were never manual workers; for example, the president of the United Packinghouse Workers is a lawyer who entered the

union as its legal counsel.   Once a national union has passed its turbulent formative period, the tenure in office of the top officers is usually very long, and often ends only with voluntary retirement.

Among the chief powers of the national officers is that of appointing the headquarters staff of the union, especially the international representatives who do much of the organizing and bargaining.   The national officers also control the content and editorial policies of union journals, which naturally report the activities of the leadership in a favorable light.

The salaries of national officers vary widely.   In a few unions with strong democratic and equalitarian traditions, the president may receive only $10,000 or $12,000 a year, perhaps twice as much as the average member.   In other unions, salaries of $40,000 to $60,000 and over are paid to the president, in addition to valuable perquisites.   The large gap between the salary of a top union officer and that of the average member prevents most union officers from returning to the shop if they are defeated and thus creates a strong motive for limiting turnover in office.   Yet it does not seem practical to advocate low salaries for top union officers as a way of promoting democracy in unions.   The job of a union president is difficult and demanding.   A president making $15,000 a year may be more capable and harder working than the corporation executive across the bargaining table from him who makes ten times this much.   A few of the more idealistic union leaders can take this disparity in stride.   Most union officers, however, even if they are of working-class origin, soon absorb middle-class values in their new role in which they have close and continuous association with middle-class people.   They come to feel that they should be paid like others who do work of similar difficulty and importance.   Nor do the members necessarily resent high salaries for their officers; on the contrary, they may take pride in the fact that their leaders who rose from the ranks can live in the same style as corporation executives.

The case of the ITU, where defeated union officers typically return to the shop, probably cannot be duplicated elsewhere. It is made possible by the high income and status of the members and by the fact that the two-party system provides activities and prestige for the leaders of the party that is out of office.

The career pattern of the union officer usually begins with election to unpaid office in a local union. Conspicuous success in such a role will lead to paid office in the local if it is large, or to a staff position in the national union. The most successful members of the national staff or outstanding leaders of large local unions are the group from which the district directors of the national union or the members of the national executive board are chosen. This structure of advancement offers a great deal of opportunity to able and ambitious members. However, the requisite for advancement, in addition to ability, is absolute loyalty to the incumbent union administration. The pattern is not unlike that of a party organization or "machine" in a large American city; the similarities include easy entry at the bottom beginning with unpaid work, and the importance of loyalty as a condition of advancement. It is perhaps because of this that the term "boss" is applied both to union leaders and to the heads of city political organizations.

It is natural for the candidates for elective offices at the national and district level to come from the paid staff, since the work of the staff both prepares it for higher office and gives it wide contacts in the membership. The selection of members of the staff to fill a vacant elective office is typically made by the incumbent officers. If a staff man has been passed over in this selection, he has the nominal right to run for election against the choice of the administration. However, if he loses, he is sure to lose his staff position (indeed, he will probably lose it when he announces his candidacy). In addition, the union newspaper and the rest of the staff will be working actively against him. It is far safer for him to bide his time and hope for another vacancy.

The few rather technical positions on a union staff (legal counsel, education director, newspaper editor, industrial engineer, etc.) are filled in a different pattern. Many union technicians are college-educated and are oriented either toward the professional standards of their occupation or toward some ideology that drew then into the union (for example, socialism or one of the religious action movements). Among such staff members, the requirement of absolute loyalty is more likely to be galling than for the man up from the ranks, and many such specialists leave the unions for government, educational institutions, or industry.[1]

§ 5. Opposition Within Trade Unions. Although only one national union has a two-party system, factions have frequently existed within national unions. In the period after World War II, almost every CIO union was split into an anti-Communist faction and a faction that included the Communists and their sympathizers. A similar factional alignment existed in the International Ladies' Garment Workers in the 1920's. In no case has this kind of factional situation proved stable. It has always ended either with the defeat and disappearance of one faction (usually the Communist faction) or with the split of the national union into two separate organizations. The instability of factions based on such fundamentally different ideologies is perhaps not surprising. However, there have also been instances of factions that can hardly be distinguished in terms of ideology, most recently in the case of the Textile Workers' Union of America, and this, too, has proved to be an unstable situation.

The basic distinction between a factional fight and a two-party system is that in the former it is assumed that the losing faction does not have the right to continued existence; it is ordered to disband on penalty of expulsion. This reflects the long tradition of opposition to "dual unionism" within the American labor movement.[2] It was often true when unions

---

[1] See Harold L. Wilensky, *Intellectuals in Labor Unions* (Glencoe, Ill.: Free Press, 1956).

[2] A recent study of dual unionism defines it as "the equivalent of the crime of treason in national states." Joel Seidman and Arlyn J. Melcher,

were weak that conflict within a union or between unions in the same industry served to worsen their bargaining position. As a result, any organized grouping of members within a union in opposition to the incumbent administration is seen as a potential dual union or as a threat to the survival and strength of the organization.

Most cases of factional fights within a union result from a division of opinion or a falling out among the leaders of the national union. In a few cases, however, protest movements originating among local union leaders have been important enough to make headway against the undivided forces of the national union leadership and staff. In the United Steel-workers of America, a union with a strong tradition of centralized leadership, an organization of dissident local leaders called the "Dues Protest Committee" made a surprisingly strong showing in a recent election for the national union presidency. The leaders of the committee after their defeat were formally brought to trial on charges of dual unionism. This suggests a rather curious concept of democratic elections in which it is permitted that one oppose an incumbent but not that there be any sort of campaign organization in behalf of the challenger.

§ 6. An Evaluation of Union Government.

The preceding sections have compared the processes of union government with the sort of democratic process found in national government in the United States. The non-unionist, and particularly the intellectual with a strong commitment to democracy, will view this comparison as an unfavorable one for the unions. It does not follow that the unionist views it in the same way. As long as a union does a good job of protecting the economic and job interests of the members, they will almost always give it full and warm support. The occasional

"The Dual Union Clause and Political Rights," *Labor Law Journal* (September, 1960). Seidman and Melcher find that clauses in union constitutions dealing with dual unionism are often very vague and give broad disciplinary powers to top union officials.

individual within an oligarchic union who attempts to protest against lack of democracy is likely to be viewed by his fellows as a crackpot or a troublemaker. Indeed, as long as a union "delivers" for the members, the members are often willing to support not only authoritarian leaders, but sometimes corrupt leaders or Communist leaders. One of the puzzling aspects of the undemocratic practices of such union leaders as James Hoffa and John L. Lewis is that they were obviously not necessary, since these leaders had overwhelming support in the membership. In general the concern about lack of democracy in unions has come from outside the unions themselves; from academic critics, from such organizations as the American Civil Liberties Union, or from political leaders. Among the unionists who are aware of them, these criticisms are suspect as being employer-inspired (as of course some of them are).

The absence of organized opposition within unions should not be taken to mean that union officers are usually unresponsive to the demands of the membership. Officers will respond to membership pressures not because they fear being voted out of office, but because they view their job as that of fighting for the members and take pride in doing this job well. While there is conflict between the leadership and potential internal opponents, there is not usually any diversity of interest between leaders and members in seeking gains in collective bargaining. To the extent that leadership views on bargaining demands and strategy differ from those of the rank and file, it is usually the leaders who are more moderate. Increasing union democracy is therefore likely to lead unions to make larger economic demands and to press grievances that have little merit.

So long as there is no strong feeling within the unions of a need for more democratic government, it will be difficult to create democracy by fiat from the outside. Legal regulation of internal union affairs is more likely to touch the forms than the substance of democracy, and in most cases the forms are already present. It may nevertheless be possible in some cases to rule out economic reprisals against dissident members or to provide them with more recourse to the civil courts. The courts have typically refused to enter cases brought by members against voluntary organizations until all avenues of internal appeal have been exhausted, a process that may take a very long time. However, there now seems to be some growing recognition of the union as a quasi-public rather than a purely voluntary organization.

One of the most promising developments in recent years in the protection of individual rights within unions has been the establishment by the United Automobile Workers of its Public Review Board in 1957. The board consists of seven members drawn from the clergy, the bar, and the universities; it acts as a court of last resort in internal appeals. As of March, 1960, the board had decided 29 cases, upholding the executive board of the union in 23 and reversing it in 6. Some of the reversals have led the union to make changes in its constitution along lines suggested by the board's decisions.[1] It is disappointing that no other large union has followed the example set by the auto workers in creating a public review board.

Because of the difficulty of imposing democracy on organizations in which it has not developed naturally, the chief contribution of public policy may be that of permitting changes in the choice of a bargaining agent. A local union in opposition to important policies of its national organization has little chance of getting them reversed. However, the procedures of the National Labor Relations Board give it an avenue for affiliating with a different national union or for becoming an independent local.

It is sometimes argued that a worker who was subject only to the authority of his employer in the pre-union period has suffered a further restriction of freedom if an authoritarian union enters the picture. This argument is of dubious validity.

[1] See Jack Stieber, Walter E. Oberer, and Michael Harrington, *Democracy and Public Review: An Analysis of the UAW Public Review Board* (Santa Barbara, Calif.: Center for the Study of Democratic Institutions, 1960).

Rivalry between a union and management may create new freedoms for workers even if both are organizations based on authority, since each protects him from abuse by the other. Only if these two institutions collude against him does his situation deteriorate. It is probably true, however, that management cannot or will not protect a man against the arbitrary use of union authority more often than a union will fail to protect him against the arbitrary use of management authority.

It is also paradoxically true that the presence of strong unions may improve the operation of democratic processes in the general national or state government even if the internal political processes of the unions are undemocratic. As they enter the larger political scene, unions represent one of a variety of contending interest groups. Where these groups are relatively numerous and equally balanced, the public interest may be better served than where a few dominate. On many issues the opposition between unions and business organizations may have helped to prevent public policy from serving the special interest of either.

§ 7. **Political Action by Unions.** American unions are not political in the same sense as unions in most other countries in that they do not have an open and permanent affiliation with one political party. Nevertheless, almost all American unions engage to some extent in efforts to influence elections and decisions in national, state, and local politics. Among the most conservative craft unions, political action is largely confined to promoting the direct economic interests of the craft or trade. A number of the leaders of such unions have been active Republicans; Martin Durkin, a leader of the plumbers' union, was the first Secretary of Labor in the Eisenhower cabinet. For the most part, however, union leaders have supported the Democratic party in the last twenty-five years, and in particular have supported the northern liberal wing of the Democratic party. This position is in part an application of the old rule that labor should support its friends and oppose its enemies, since the northern Democrats have typically fought legislation that would restrict or regulate unions, while Republicans and southern Democrats have generally supported such legislation. The position of union leaders and of northern Democrats has also tended to be similar on issues not directly affecting unions, such as taxation, housing, monetary policy, and social security.

The political position of unions as a whole is that of favoring increased state intervention in the economy through extension of such programs as social security, public housing, public power, minimum wage laws, and the like, but not extending to the large-scale public ownership of mining, manufacturing, or distributive industries.   In fighting for such things as improved unemployment insurance programs or the use of income taxes rather than sales taxes in financing state and local governments, the unions represent the interest of a group much broader than their own membership.   On many of these issues, they are the only effective lobby representing low-income urban people, for there are no strong political organizations of consumers or of non-union workers.   Although the positions taken by unions on particular issues may not always be in the interest of the community as a whole, at least as it is construed by other groups, it does seem to be in the public interest to have some strong group that will act as the champion of the underdog.

Many of the measures that unions have supported are in the immediate economic interests of union members.   Others, however, represent a more general ideological position whose application in particular areas works against the short-run interests of the members.   Thus unions have backed high price supports for agricultural commodities, a position that is contrary to the immediate interests of union members both as consumers of farm products and as workers in the industries that process and distribute them.

The AFL–CIO maintains a Washington staff to present labor's position to Congress and to the administrative agencies of the federal government.   In addition, most large national unions maintain Washington representatives for this purpose, and several major unions have their national headquarters in Washington. The AFL–CIO state organizations usually maintain similar offices at state capitals. At the local level such unions as the building trades, which are vitally affected by local building codes and licensing laws, maintain close contact with local political organizations.

The effectiveness of any lobby depends not so much on the cogency of its arguments as on its ability to deliver votes, money, or both to party organizations or candidates. Unions typically endorse candidates for office and attempt to persuade their members to vote for them. Ordinarily the endorsement is made not by the unions as such, but by a subsidiary body of the AFL–CIO, the Committee on Political Education (COPE). COPE usually endorses Democrats and union members usually vote for Democrats. However, this is not good evidence of the success of COPE; there is a strong coincidence of natural preferences between the unions and their members, arising from the well-known differences in party preference by socioeconomic class (outside the South). The union member typically votes Democratic because of the traditions of his family, his ethnic group, or his neighborhood rather than because the union urges him to, and many loyal union members have doubts about the right of unions to make political endorsements. When a union leader attempts to sway his members against their natural inclination, he almost always fails. The most celebrated case is that of John L. Lewis, who in 1940 supported Wendell Willkie for president against Franklin D. Roosevelt and who resigned as president of the CIO when it became apparent that CIO members had overwhelmingly ignored his position in casting their ballots. The effectiveness of union political activity therefore lies largely in getting union members registered and in seeing that they remember to vote rather than in persuading them to alter their positions.

Unions support candidates by articles, editorials, and cartoons in union papers; by programs at union meetings; by having union staff do precinct work; and by contributing money to campaign funds. The Taft-Hartley Law prohibits the use of dues funds for contributions to candidates for federal office, so that voluntary contributions are collected to support such candidates. At the state and local level, contributions are made from union treasuries.

In some states, unions have played an important part in the internal affairs of the Democratic party, though there is probably only one case (Michigan) where unions have had anything resembling control of a major political party at the state level. Even in Michigan, where union influence in politics has reached its highest level, union leaders have usually not done well as candidates for public office. The members of unions are still a minority in the electorate in the most highly industrialized states. Unions have been most successful when they have supported someone sympathetic with their position who has not been a career union leader.[1]

The role of unions in politics has long seemed a menacing one to American conservatives, probably because they have typically overrated its effectiveness. Yet the major farm and business interests have always played an important political role, and it was only natural for unions to seek to do likewise. Perhaps it would be good for American democracy if economic interest groups all stayed out of politics, though this is surely debateable. It does seem clear, however, that if some producer groups are to have strong political influence, it is best for the consumer for all of them to have influence. Since consumers have seldom had an effective lobby of their own, they may get some protection from conflicts of interest among producer lobbies.

It would be highly unfortunate for American democracy if any part of the electorate came to feel that the machinery of government did not permit its interests to be adequately represented, so that it felt it necessary to oppose the system

---

[1] One of the best studies of union political activity is Fay Calkins, *The CIO and the Democratic Party* (Chicago: University of Chicago Press, 1952). This book includes a study of the role of the CIO in Michigan.

of government as a whole. The participation of unions in politics can help to prevent workers from developing such a feeling, and thus can inhibit the growth of anti-democratic political movements among workers.

CHAPTER XI

CORRUPTION IN UNIONS

§ 1. Background. Corruption and labor racketeering have long been present in some American unions. Extensive investigations by a Senate Committee (the McClellan Committee) and the expulsion of a major union (the teamsters) from the AFL–CIO on charges of corruption have brought the problem into sharp focus in the last few years.

Corruption in unions takes a number of forms: Union funds have been embezzled or misappropriated to private uses by union officers. Officers have received valuable gifts and interest-free loans (often not repaid) from employers, presumably in return for concessions at the bargaining table. Insurance contracts of union health and welfare funds have been placed with agencies in which union officers had a financial interest. Union officers have turned up as the principal owners of firms with which their unions bargained. In some cases, local unions have been fronts for men with long criminal records; these men have organized associations that were unions only in name and that extorted money from employers.

The revelations of the McClellan Committee have been viewed in different ways by different parts of the community. Unions point out that corruption has always been widespread in many parts of American life, including notoriously local politics, and that almost every instance of union corruption involves also connivance or tacit consent by some element in the business community. Not long after the issues of union corruption were in the news, scandals involving fraud and bribery ("payola") in the radio and television industry took their place in the headlines. Embezzlement is far more common among bank employees than among union employees. Corruption in unions has also been viewed as a part of a broader characteristic of American culture by observers from the upright countries of Northern Europe.[1]

When all this has been said, however, it must be admitted that the traditions of the union movement gave reason for expecting a higher standard of morality among union leaders than among disc jockeys or ward committeemen. That this hope was not wholly vain is shown by the fact that the unions with a heritage of radicalism or broad concern for social welfare have been the unions where corruption has been conspicuously absent. Virtually no corruption has been found in the unions of the old CIO or in such welfare-minded unions of the old AF of L as the International Ladies' Garment Workers' Union, though a few unsavory episodes involving such unions have occurred when professional gangsters moved in and took control of locals. The corrupt national unions have been almost entirely in the tradition of pure and simple business unionism.

Employers and conservative spokesmen are inclined to view corruption in unions as an outcome of excessive union power. When a union has great power to raise wages, they argue, it has a source of personal gain that leaders will be tempted to tap. This relationship between economic power and corruption deserves exploration. While it is by no means true that all unions with substantial power over relative wages are corrupt, there is reason to believe that many corrupt unions have such power.

§ 2. The Relation between Economic Power and Corruption.
To determine whether economic power is a necessary condition

[1] See for example B. C. Roberts, *Unions in America: A British View* (Princeton: Industrial Relations Section, Princeton University, 1959), Chapter IV.

for corruption in unions, we must specify the kind of corruption involved. Clearly, ordinary embezzlement can occur in any business that handles money, even if it operates under conditions of pure competition. Thus a clerk in a grocery store can rob the till, and the store insures against this by bonding its clerks. The costs of bonding become part of the normal costs of doing business in the industry. Exactly the same model is applicable to a union with no power over wages; such a union receives dues from its members in return for performing the non-wage functions of collective bargaining or in return for an imagined power over wages that does not actually exist. The union may also receive money as contributions to pension or welfare funds. The union employees or officers who handle finances are subject to the same kind of temptations as the grocery clerk and are therefore normally bonded. The cost of the bond becomes part of the costs of the business of providing collective bargaining services.

The cases of union corruption that fit the model above are probably the less important cases—those that involve minor employees rather than the top leadership and those that involve isolated incidents rather than the general tone of the organization. Pervasive, large-scale corruption does seem to involve prior economic power. If a union had no power to raise relative wages and if nevertheless the officers took very large amounts by misappropriating dues, the net relative wages of the members would be somewhat below the competitive level. Such a union might be open to raiding by other unions and its officers would be more vulnerable to internal revolt. The principal source of any private gains by the officers would have to be dues revenues or welfare funds, since if they did not have the power to make wage gains from employers, they presumably also would have little power to exact money from employers for their own benefit. (1)

On the other hand, in a union with power to make large economic gains, the opportunities for corruption are always present. Satisfaction of the membership with the economic performance of the union contributes to oligarchy and long (2) tenure in office, which reduce the possibility that corruption will be detected. Officers who have been highly successful in winning gains for the members may even retain strong membership support after corruption has been exposed, in part because manual workers have a less rigid respect for the law than the middle class. (There is still some basis for the Marxist sneer "bourgeois morality.")

The leader of a union with economic power can receive private payments either from employers or from the membership. The members are usually the losers in either case, since in an honest union an equal ability to get payments from employers would be used to raise wages. The device employed to get payments from the members is union control of hiring, where there is no objective method used to determine priority in referring members to jobs. For example, the notorious International Longshoremen's Association on the East Coast long used the shape-up system of hiring, in which workers lined up on the docks each day to receive work and the men hired were selected by an agent of the union. Because in part of the union's success in raising wages there was always an oversupply of applicants and the men chosen were expected to kick back part of their wage. In New York and New Jersey, the shape-up system has now been ended by state law. The ILA was expelled from the AFL–CIO for corruption, but a rival AFL–CIO union organized to take its place has made little headway in NLRB elections.

A corrupt union leader can get private payments from employers in return for a substandard contract (a so-called "sweetheart agreement") or in return for settling or averting a strike that would impose losses on the firm. In some cases unions are organized for the sole purpose of obtaining a sweetheart agreement and never perform any of the day-to-day functions of collective bargaining. Some such corrupt unions pretend to be plant level independents; other are locals of national unions. Employers sometimes assist in organizing such a union to forestall organization by a legitimate union. This is of course a violation of the federal labor relations laws

and if it is detected the union will not be certified as the
bargaining agent.

If a corrupt union has the power to impose a wage, say, of
15 cents an hour above the prevailing level, the temptation is
to split the difference three ways. A wage increase of 8 cents
per hour will perhaps convince the members that their union
has won a good contract; a side payment equivalent to 2 cents
an hour could amount to a large sum for the corrupt leaders,
and a wage saving of 5 cents an hour might convince an
unscrupulous employer to enter such an agreement.

It may be noted that the preceding paragraph implies that
the corrupt union has a smaller adverse effect on the allocation
of resources than the honest union. The saving in labor cost
to the employer under a "sweetheart agreement" gives him a
smaller incentive to economize in the use of union labor than
exists for the employer dealing with an honest union. The
difference is even larger if the payments to the corrupt union
leaders are lump sums not related to employment, since such
a lump sum "tax" will also leave the determination of hours
and employment unaffected. One would like to hope that
there are not many circumstances where honesty and efficiency
are thus opposed.

It is interesting to consider the special case in which the
dishonest union leader has greater bargaining skills than any
honest rival, and the best settlement that could be won by an
honest leader selected from this membership would be only
8 cents an hour in the example used above. In this case the
employed members do not lose anything from the dishonesty,
and the leader could justify his corrupt income as payment for
his unusual skill. Such situations might result from the
traditions of low salaries for officers in some unions. However, it seems in general to be true that the unions where there
is corruption are also the unions that pay high salaries and
generous expense allowances to officers or business agents.
This case illustrates the dilemma of the advocate of honesty
and democracy in unions. If he insists on low salaries for
skilled negotiators to promote turnover in office and to increase

the chance that former officers will return to the shop, he increases the temptations to dishonesty.

The extent of corruption in unions, since corruption involves employer knowledge or acquiescence in most cases, may also depend on the characteristics of the employers with which a union deals. The best target is the small employer in a highly competitive industry, for whom a slight difference in labor cost may be important to survival and who does not have the resources to fight a powerful union. Large firms are better able to resist participation in corrupt partnerships with union leaders and either have higher standards of morality or greater fear of exposure (since they are more vulnerable to adverse public opinion). This difference may help to explain why the corrupt unions have been highly concentrated in the local market industries. There is, however, at least one very large firm (a mail order house) whose relationships with a union leader were shown by the McClellan Committee to be of doubtful morality, to say the least.

§ 3. **Dealing with Corruption.** The traditional position of the labor movement on dealing with corruption has been that this is something labor must do for itself, and that public intervention is not needed. In line with this position the AFL–CIO created an Ethical Practices Committee headed by President Hayes of the machinists. The work of this committee has caused some small unions in the AFL–CIO to clean up their affairs rather than risk expulsion from the federation. Several national unions have been expelled, and new rival nationals have been created to compete with some of these. The new unions have had considerable success in some cases, notably in the bakery industry. However, the fundamental problem of the AFL–CIO is illustrated by the expulsions of the International Longshoremen's Association (from the old AF of L) and the teamsters. In the first case the new rival national union had very limited success; in the second, no attempt to organize a rival was made. It is hard to see that the expulsion of the teamsters has hurt them at all, while it has cost the AFL–CIO a considerable amount of revenue and perhaps some valuable support of its affiliates in strike situations (since such support is obtained at the local level, it is hard to tell just what difference expulsion has made.)

It is because of the failure of internal reform in such instances that Congress passed the Landrum-Griffin Act by a wide margin. Key provisions of this act are designed to reduce corruption in trade unions, in large part by requiring strict financial reporting. The unions opposed the passage of the act in its final form, although they had supported milder and more restricted bills containing financial reporting requirements. In the twenty-four years between the Wagner Act and the Landrum-Griffin Act, Congress has abandoned the view that unions are inherently good organizations whose internal affairs need no public policing. The special immunities of unions are being replaced by regulation similar to that long applied to corporations (the closest analogy is probably the Securities and Exchange Commission as a regulator of corporate financial reporting). It would be idle to expect the first attempt at such legislation to solve all the problems or to fail to create some new ones. The principle seems firmly established, however, that the public has an interest in honesty within unions, and that the government regretfully and perhaps belatedly recognizes that power can corrupt in unions as it can everywhere else.

(2)

CHAPTER XII

EVALUATION AND PREDICTION

§ **1. The Role of the Union in American Society.** Few social or economic institutions as old and as important as the union are still as controversial. The economic impact of the union is a subject for spirited debate among economists; the nature of public policy toward the union is still an important issue in many political campaigns. It is inevitable that anyone writing about such a controversial institution will select his materials and interpret them in accordance with his own values. My own attitude toward unions has undoubtedly been apparent during much of the preceding discussion. However, an explicit statement of it here may help to prevent misinterpretation of some parts of this book.

(1)   If the union is viewed solely in terms of its effect on the economy, it must in my opinion be considered an obstacle to the optimum performance of our economic system. It alters the wage structure in a way that impedes the growth of employment in sectors of the economy where productivity and income are naturally high and that leaves too much labor in low-income sectors of the economy like southern agriculture and the least skilled service trades. It benefits most those workers who would in any case be relatively well off, and while some of this gain may be at the expense of the owners of capital, most of it must be at the expense of consumers and the lower-paid workers. Unions interfere blatantly with the use of the most productive techniques in some industries, and this effect

is probably not offset by the stimulus to higher productivity furnished by some other unions.

Many of my fellow economists would stop at this point and conclude that unions are harmful and that their power should be curbed. I do not agree that one can judge the value of a complex institution from so narrow a point of view. Other aspects of unions must also be considered The protection against the abuse of managerial authority given by seniority systems and grievance procedures seems to me to be a union accomplishment of the greatest importance. So too is the organized representation in public affairs given the worker by the political activities of unions. If, as most of us believe, America should continue to have political democracy and a free enterprise economy, it is essential that the great mass of manual workers be committed to the preservation of this system and that they should not, as in many other democracies, constantly be attempting to replace it with something radically different. Yet such a commitment cannot exist if workers feel that their rights are not respected and they do not get their fair share of the rewards of the system. By giving workers protection against arbitrary treatment by employers, by acting as their representative in politics, and by reinforcing their hope of continuous future gain, unions have helped to assure that the basic values of our society are widely diffused and that our disagreements on political and economic issues take place within a broad framework of agreement. If the job rights won for workers by unions are not conceded by the rest of society simply because they are just, they should be conceded because they help to protect the minimum consensus that keeps our society stable. In my judgment, the economic losses imposed by unions are not too high a price to pay for their successful performance of this role.

(2)

To be sure, the non-economic aspects of trade unionism could be viewed with much more complete approval if there were less corruption and more democracy in unions. The broad approval of our system of collective bargaining does not imply that there is not need for reform in many particulars, either through voluntary change within unions or through the further development of public policy. At this level, it again becomes essential to recognize the vast differences among American trade unions and to seek policies, private and public, that will encourage the best features of the union movement while discouraging others. The task is difficult, because good and bad features are often embodied in the same organization. Thus the International Typographical Union, a model of internal democracy, is wedded to costly restrictive practices like the setting of bogus, while the United Mine Workers, one of the most autocratic of American unions, has never blocked the mechanization of its industry and has pioneered in bringing good medical care to isolated mining towns.

In judging such a checkered picture, it is not possible to make sweeping generalizations. Policy toward unions must feel its way slowly, avoiding radical change for fear of throwing out the good with the bad. To the greatest extent possible, it must take advantage of those tendencies within the trade union movement that work in the general interest. In recent years, the development of policy and attitudes toward unions has in fact been this kind of cautious process. It does not differ greatly from the development of policy toward monopoly in product markets. Economic theory states unequivocally that monopoly distorts the allocation of resources. Yet most economists have approved a policy that merely restrains the growth of monopoly or nibbles at it around the edges, rather than advocating a policy of large-scale dissolution of monopolistic enterprises. This caution has several sources: for example, the fear of interfering with private property rights acquired in good faith and the fear that bigness, though associated with inefficient allocation, may also be associated with efficient management and rapid innovation. In guiding policies toward big enterprises and strong unions, economic theory can indicate the directions in which greater efficiency lies. It cannot by itself tell to what extent it is possible by deliberate social surgery and grafting to improve the performance of institutions that are the product of long evolution.

There are grave dangers in doing nothing about waste and the growth of unchecked power; there are also dangers that unwise treatment can be worse than the disease. One of the first steps in forming a framework for policy is to attempt to predict the natural development of unions in the years ahead.

§ 2. The Future Growth of Unions. In the years from 1933 to 1945, unionism swept the manual workers of the United States. Aided by friendly public policy and by a spirit of radicalism growing out of the miserable performance of the economy in the 1930's, American unionism changed from a movement of the craft elite to a movement that embraced the great majority of workers in manufacturing, mining, construction, and transporation, except in the South. After 1945, unions stopped gaining important new territory and grew largely because employment grew in the industries already organized. Since 1953, employment of manual workers has ceased to grow in the highly organized sectors of the economy as automation and related technological developments have made possible increasing output with a reduction in employment. From 1953 to 1960, the Federal Reserve Board index of production for manufacturing rose from 92.1 to 108.2 (1957=100). Over the same period, the number of wage and salary workers in manufacturing fell from 17.2 million to 16.3 million, and the fall took place entirely in the number of production workers. In mining, too, there were increases in output combined with decreases in employment. The growth in employment since 1953 has taken place almost entirely in trade, finance, services, and government, the areas of the economy where unions are weakest. The impact of the change has been felt by a number of the manufacturing unions, who have lost membership and have had to reduce their staffs. If unionism remains confined to manual workers, it seems destined to represent a smaller portion of the labor force than it does at present, for the technological developments that underlie the shifting industrial and occupational composition of employment do not yet seem to have run their course.

(A)

(1)

(2)

(3)

(B)

Unions can hold their present relative strength only if they succeed in organizing white-collar and technical workers to a much larger extent than in the past. But here the exposure of widespread corruption in unions has hurt them much more than it has among their present members. Secretaries and engineers are far less likely to condone the use of force and the misuse of funds by union leaders than are teamsters and long-shoremen. Two more basic factors also work against the unionization of the white-collar worker, and unions have seldom been able to overcome them on a large scale. At the lower levels of white-collar employment, most of the workers are women. If they are married or expect to get married, work occupies a less important part of their lives than it does for men. Young women and married women tend to leave the labor force, or to move in and out, and to stay with one employer for a relatively short time. It is hard to organize a union in such a work force and to keep it organized; successful organization requires that the worker have a large stake in improving the conditions of his job. At the higher levels of white-collar work, the second difficulty arises. The white-collar employee sees his future in terms of upward mobility within the management hierarchy; he identifies with manage-ment and adopts management's cool or hostile attitude toward unions. To be sure, where management does not handle its personnel problems wisely in white-collar employment, unions can overcome these natural obstacles. Several firms that employ large numbers of engineers and give them little chance for individual recognition and advancement have been shocked to see the unionization of their engineers. However, manage-ment is spending large amounts for the improvement of policies toward white-collar personnel; if the art of personnel adminis-tration has any merit, the worst mistakes should usually be avoided.

The unions have lost another less obvious source of strength; the many able, idealistic, well-educated people who in the thirties and forties flocked into careers in the union movement. Unions at that time represented an exciting social frontier, and pioneering spirits wanted to work at the frontier. Though many of them got no further than turning the mimeograph machine or carrying a picket sign, others became research directors, editors, lawyers, organizers, and even union officers. There has been widespread disillusionment in this group, and in the group that might furnish their successors. The change can be seen in the kinds of students who study industrial relations in the universities. Fifteen years ago, many liberal arts students who looked forward to a union career were attracted to courses in labor. Today these courses are increasingly filled by students who expect a career in the personnel departments of companies or in teaching and who are motivated by opportunities for advancement and security rather than by opportunities for service and adventure. If this change reflects what has happened to the universities as much as what has happened to the unions, it nevertheless represents a loss to the labor movement. Unions will continue to get ability by growing it in the ranks or buying it in the market, but missionary zeal will be harder to find.

None of this means that unions are likely to lose the full support of the groups that furnish their present strength. I know of no evidence whatever of the defection of any important group of unionists from the union movement. Such dissatisfactions as exist with particular unions are almost always expressed in a desire to be in a different union rather than in none. What does seem clear, however, is that unions will be a smaller minority in the society as a whole than they have been, and one with fewer and less reliable allies, especially among the intellectuals.

conclusion

There also seems to be a growing determination in management to make fewer concessions to unions; to "bargain harder" than in the past, and to get something in return for what is given. Such a determination was evident in management's attitude in the steel strike of 1959, and although the settlement of that particular strike was hardly a victory for management, the stance adopted may promise fewer easy victories for unions in years to come.

§ 3. The Trend in Internal Union Affairs.

We have seen that as unions change from new and struggling organizations to successful, long-established ones, they tend to become bureaucratic in their internal political structure, and that in this they are like most private voluntary organizations. They are also likely to become more "responsible" in their dealings with management, to be more cautious in the use of the strike, more temperate in their public utterances, and perhaps less extreme in their demands. The union leader is less likely to think of himself as a fighter and more likely to aspire to be a labor statesman and a leader of the community. From time to time we can expect to see temporary reversals of this trend in one union or another, but no forces are in sight that promise to reverse it generally.

The public regulation of unions could remove some of the blatant abuses of democratic procedures and some of the less subtle kinds of corruption. However, this seems to promise not the revival of the lusty immature union of the 1930's, but rather a more respectable kind of maturity. If public policy should help to eliminate the racketeering union (and it is by no means certain that it can) and if the radical union also disappears, the union movement will continue to become more homogeneous. The demise of the radical union seems certain; only a few unions still have Communist leadership, and in these the leaders are increasingly not free to state their positions on general political issues. As the Communist party loses its sources of support among intellectuals and workers alike, there is less and less likelihood that the leaders of these unions will be succeeded by other men of the same views. Perhaps it will eventually be possible for unions like the United Electrical Workers, once ousted from the CIO for its Communist leanings, to be reabsorbed in the AFL–CIO union in its industry.

The occasional revival of the exuberant, irresponsible unionism of the past depends largely on the possibility of occasional revolt by the rank and file against the stodginess of an entrenched leadership. In this connection it must be remarked that the devotion of management spokesmen to the use of democratic processes in unions is either a tribute to their political philosophy or a reflection on their powers of observation, for it has been demonstrated repeatedly that the rank and file is more extravagent in its demands and less understanding of the problems of management, except where there is an obvious threat to employment, than are well-established union leaders.

§ **4. The Development of Public Policy.**   Public policy toward unions in the United States has gone through a number of phases.   Before 1932, the policy was one of hostile toleration; the right of unions to exist and to strike was recognized, yet the law placed many serious obstacles in the path of successful organization.   From 1932 to about 1945, the policy was one of the active encouragement of organization and of government support for many union bargaining demands.   Since 1945, the trend has been increasingly toward neutrality.   The right of workers to organize and to bargain collectively continues to be firmly protected.   However, public policy has been increasingly concerned with the rights of workers to stay out of unions if they choose, with the rights of minorities within unions, with the restriction of certain bargaining practices that are considered unfair, and with the protection of the general public against the consequences of emergency strikes.

It would be impossible to predict the specific ways in which public policy toward unions is likely to develop from now on. However, the general framework seems reasonably well set. The basic right of workers to bargain collectively is now more widely accepted than ever before, and those who hold that unions are fundamentally alien to the American political and economic system are a vanishing minority.   At the same time, there are now many fewer people than there were twenty years ago who feel that unions can do no wrong.   Thus it seems clear that public policy will continue to encourage unionism but at the same time to view it watchfully and to regulate its operation.

For thirteen years unions tried to win the repeal of the hated Taft-Hartley Act, which they called a slave labor law. By failing to support compromise revisions, they ended with the law basically unchanged. On the issue of corruption, unions were willing to support some legislation, but nothing as far-reaching as the Landrum-Griffin Act. It seems clear that in the future the issues will involve give and take about particulars rather than sharp divisions of principle about the right of the public to regulate collective bargaining and internal union affairs.

But even as public policy is helping to shape the future of the unions, unions are helping to shape public policy in areas far removed from collective bargaining. By proposing or supporting such measures as aid to chronically depressed areas and publicly financed medical care for the aged, unions are acting as a social conscience for the American economy. The particular positions advocated are often too extreme to be accepted. Yet by raising such issues and keeping them alive the unions assure that in our satisfaction with the general growth and stability of the economy, we will not become complacent about groups that are getting left behind. It is in this role of social conscience more than in the role of collective bargainer that the labor movement still plays Robin Hood.

INDEX